# EXODUS
## — W I T H I N —
# BORDERS

# EXODUS
## —WITHIN—
# BORDERS

## An Introduction to the Crisis
## of Internal Displacement

**David A. Korn**

BROOKINGS INSTITUTION PRESS
Washington, D.C.

ABOUT BROOKINGS

The Brookings Institution is a private nonprofit organization devoted to research, education, and publication on important issues of domestic and foreign policy. Its principal purpose is to bring knowledge to bear on current and emerging policy problems. The Institution maintains a position of neutrality on issues of public policy. Interpretations or conclusions in Brookings publications should be understood to be solely those of the authors.

*Library of Congress Cataloging-in-Publication data*
Korn, David A.
      Exodus within borders : an introduction to the crisis of internal
displacement / David A. Korn
        p. cm.
      Includes bibliographical references and index.
      ISBN 0-8157-4954-6 (cloth : alk. paper)
      ISBN 0-8157-4953-8 (pbk : alk. paper)
      1. Humanitarian assistance. 2. Forced migration. 3. Migration, Internal.
I. Title.
      HV544.5 .K67 1998
      307.2—dc21                                                    98-40261
                                                                        CIP

First softcover printing January, 2000

9  8  7  6  5  4  3  2

The paper used in this publication meets the minimum requirements of the American National Standard for Information Sciences—Permanence of Paper for Printed Library Materials: ANSI Z39.48-1984.

Typeset in Minion and Gill Sans
Design and composition by Harlowe Typography, Cottage City, Maryland
Printed by R. R. Donnelley & Sons, Harrisonburg, Virginia

# Foreword

**T**his brief volume of text and photographs is based on the in-depth study *Masses in Flight: The Global Crisis of Internal Displacement* by Roberta Cohen and Francis M. Deng. The title of the book is drawn from an article by Cohen and Deng in *Foreign Affairs* (July-August 1998). The book and its companion volume, *The Forsaken People: Case Studies of the Internally Displaced*, were undertaken at the suggestion of former UN Secretary-General Boutros Boutros-Ghali, in the aim of helping the international community determine how best to organize itself to deal with the humanitarian, political, and economic problems raised by large-scale internal displacement. The current work grew out of a suggestion by UN Secretary-General Kofi Annan to Francis Deng to make available to a broader public, in summary and less technical form, the essential findings of the earlier studies. And through photographs to give an idea, more vividly perhaps than is possible through words alone, of just what it means to be driven from one's home with no sure place of refuge.

The text of the current volume was prepared by David A. Korn, writer and former diplomat. Photographs were in the main provided by the renowned Paris-based Brazilian photographer Sebastiao Salgado; Hiram Ruiz, policy analyst for Latin America and Asia for the U.S. Committee for Refugees and a talented photographer in his own right; and staff members of the UN High Commissioner for Refugees: A. Hollmann, R. Le Moyne, R. Redmond, L. Taylor, and W. van de Linde. Other photographic contributors were Roger P. Winter, executive director of the U.S. Committee for Refugees; Philippe Dutoit of the International Committee of the Red Cross; Maria Stavropoulou, formerly of the UN Centre for Human Rights; Jennifer McLean Marsh of the Brookings Institution; and Médecins Sans Frontières, the UN Economic Commission for Africa, the UN Department of Public Information, and the International Organization for Migration. To all the Brookings Institution extends warmest thanks.

Through the photographs and the text, it is hoped to foster better public understanding both of the severity of the tragedy of internal displacement and the means through which the international community can act to alleviate it.

The financial support of funders is gratefully acknowledged. The Brookings Institution Project on Internal Displacement has received generous support from the John D. and Catherine T. MacArthur Foundation, the McKnight Foundation, and the governments of the Netherlands, Norway, and Sweden.

James Schneider edited the manuscript, Eloise Stinger proofread it, and Bruce Tracy compiled the index.

The views expressed in this book are those of the author and of the authors of *Masses in Flight*. They should not be ascribed to those persons or organizations whose assistance is acknowledged or to the trustees, officers, or other staff members of the Brookings Institution.

Michael H. Armacost
*President*

*November 1998*
*Washington, D.C.*

# Contents

# EXODUS

## —WITHIN—

# BORDERS

# Introduction

They lit the torch
and threw it into
the house, laughing.
They said if we did
not leave, they
would come back
and not leave even
the dogs alive. Then
we left, without
taking anything, only
odds and ends.

Cited in Jennifer Bailey,
*The Mustard Seed,* Jesuit
Refugee Service/USA,
Spring 1997

On a day in February 1996 in the northern department of Cesar in Colombia, a group of heavily armed men pulled peasants from their homes, beat them with whips, and set fire to a school and other buildings. The men gave the peasants an ultimatum: abandon your land within five days or pay the price with your lives. Alhough an army base and a national police station were within a few kilometers, the authorities ignored the peasants' pleas for help. In fear for their lives, 280 families fled.

Had these people been able to cross a border to a neighboring state, they would have become refugees. As refugees, they would have been eligible for assistance from the international community in the collective person of the UN High Commissioner for Refugees (UNHCR), an organization with a staff of more than 5,000 and a $1.22 billion annual budget. Depending on the circumstances UNHCR would have defended their right to asylum; offered them emergency shelter, food, medical care, and rehabilitation assistance; and ultimately helped them make a safe return to and resettlement in their country and area of origin. But there was no border within reach for the peasant farmers of the

Colombian department of Cesar, and they were too poor even to consider the possibility of traveling far. So they are assumed to have dispersed into the surrounding municipalities, joining the ranks of the country's estimated 600,000 to 1,000,000 cruelly destitute internally displaced persons.

The Refugee Convention of 1951, supplemented and strengthened by the 1967 Refugee Protocol, gives the international community legal authority, through the intermediary of UNHCR, to protect and assist refugees. No international organization has parallel authority to intervene on behalf of the tens of millions of persons, across four continents, who have been uprooted from their homes and livelihoods in the past decade but who did not cross a border. They—the internally displaced—fall under the sovereign authority of their governments, which, if not actually their persecutors, may be unable or unwilling to help them. No organization or group can be counted on automatically to come to their assistance. Even the International Committee of the Red Cross (ICRC) is authorized only to protect civilians in clearly recognized situations of armed conflict.

Yet the internally displaced are the single largest at-risk population in the world. They are beset by hunger, disease, and lack of adequate shelter. They are abused both by governments and insurgent forces and suffer mortality rates of epidemic proportions. Tens of millions of people on all continents, driven from their homes, have been caught within the borders of their own countries with no international authority to which to turn for assistance and protection.

In recent years the international community has moved, first hesitantly and later with growing determination, to organize itself to remedy the shortcomings in international assistance and protection for the internally displaced. In 1992, at the request of the UN Commission on Human Rights, Secretary-General Boutros Boutros-Ghali appointed Francis M. Deng, senior fellow at the

Brookings Institution and former Sudanese ambassador and minister of state for foreign affairs, as his representative on internally displaced persons. Over the course of the decade UN humanitarian and development agencies came to recognize the internally displaced as a distinct category of persons requiring attention. In 1994 the UN emergency relief coordinator (ERC) was formally designated as "reference point" for requests for assistance and protection in situations of internal displacement. In his 1997 UN reform program, Secretary-General Kofi Annan reaffirmed the responsibility of the ERC for ensuring that protection and assistance for internally displaced persons are addressed.

These advances notwithstanding, assistance to the internally displaced is still largely ad hoc, carried out case by case with each agency doing what it believes it can and should do. And protection for internally displaced populations has remained even more of a problem, with serious situations still left unattended.

It might be said that the internally displaced forced themselves on the attention of the world. For it is the enormous growth in their numbers and in the number of countries suffering significant problems of internal displacement that gave impetus to the change in attitude toward them. A decade and a half ago, there were thought to be no more than a few million persons internally displaced in only half a dozen countries. Today the total number is estimated at between 20 million and 25 million in some forty countries, substantially more than the 13 million refugees that UNHCR recognizes as falling within its mandate.

Beyond its obvious humanitarian and human rights aspects, internal displacement also raises serious problems for the international economic and political order. Only infrequently do the crises that generate this displacement remain confined to a single country. More commonly, massive internal displacement becomes the spark that ignites refugee flows. And refugees, it turns out, are no longer so welcome as they were during much of the cold war

**Internally displaced persons in Sierra Leone carry what belongings they can gather to a temporary shelter.**

Photograph by Hiram Ruiz, U.S. Committee for Refugees.

era, when they came mainly from the Soviet bloc. Then the Western powers had a political interest in throwing open the gates to those who fled from Soviet oppression; and the refugees arrived in relatively manageable numbers. Since the end of the cold war the numbers have mushroomed while the unique political motivation of that earlier time has vanished. Western governments and those in other parts of the world have become reluctant to take in large numbers of refugees. Assisting and protecting persons displaced within their own countries keeps them from becoming refugees.

But even when crises of internal displacement remain largely confined within the borders of a single country, as in Colombia, they may cause severe economic and political disruption. The violence and instability that spark internal displacement often infect neighboring states and spread through entire regions. The worst situations can require international armed intervention.

Although instances of large internal displacements almost always arise from complex causes, all can be said to reflect a breakdown in the basic mechanisms of society and, to one extent or another, a crisis of national identity. Let us first look briefly at this common element.

# Chapter One

# A Crisis of National Identity

... ethnicity is clearly a resource for political manipulation and entrepreneurship.

Francis M. Deng, "Ethnicity: An African Predicament," *Brookings Review* (Summer 1997).

When UN Secretary-General Boutros Boutros-Ghali was asked by the Commission on Human Rights to appoint a representative on internally displaced persons, his first choice was Francis M. Deng. The secretary-general called Deng in the spring of 1992. He did not ask him to consider the assignment; he said he wanted him for it and made clear that the only answer he would accept was yes. Deng had a reputation both as diplomat and scholar, but Boutros-Ghali explained that he had another reason as well for choosing him. Deng was the scion of a leading family of Sudan's Dinka people who have suffered massive displacement from civil war. He would, as Boutros-Ghali put it, "know what the problem is all about."

Although the position is voluntary and part time, since his appointment Deng has visited countries with acute problems of internal displacement in Africa, Asia, Europe, and Latin America. In each he has met with government officials, international and nongovernmental organizations, community and religious leaders, and the displaced themselves, seeking to probe the causes of displacement and identify remedies. Circumstances have varied widely from country to country, but in virtually every case Deng found a common denominator in what he calls "a crisis of national identity," a crisis, he points out, "that generates cleavages between the affected population and the controlling authorities, governments, or insurgent groups."

The concept was crystalized for him by a remark made by a woman in a group he met while visiting a camp for internally displaced persons in the eastern region of Tajikistan, the poorest and most remote of the now independent former Soviet republics of Central Asia. He was looking for ways to help resettle and reintegrate the more than half million of Tajikistan's six million population uprooted by the civil war that broke out there in 1991. He asked the group what message they would like him to take to the country's leaders when he returned to the capital. There was a silence, almost as though the question had not come through clearly in translation. Then a woman spoke up to answer: "We have no leaders there."

Time and again on his country missions Deng has heard this same simple but profoundly meaningful message. For the internally displaced the government was not their government; it represented an alien, competing, and often hostile racial, linguistic, religious, cultural, or tribal group. For governments—not all but many—the displaced, although citizens in theory, have been regarded as an alien and threatening group, usually with a different language, culture, or religion, and most often a minority subjected to abusive rule by the majority. The common complaint of each side is "These are not our people."

This sense of alienation defined in terms of race, ethnicity, language, culture, or religion Deng has found to be present to some extent in virtually every major case of forced displacement. The divisions it causes undermine national unity. They make illusory any sense of political or social solidarity. In many instances the crisis of national identity is open and apparent for all to see:

**Francis Deng addresses a gathering of internally displaced persons during a visit to Peru in 1995.**

Photograph by Maria Stavropoulou.

in Rwanda and Burundi between Tutsis and Hutus; in Sudan between the Arabized Muslim north and the more indigenous African south; in the former Yugoslavia among Muslims, Serbs, and Croats; in Sri Lanka between Sinhalese and Tamils; in Turkey between Turks and Kurds.

Even when displacement appears to be about other issues altogether, the identity factor is clearly present. In Somalia, one of Africa's few racially and linguistically homogenous countries, identity based on clan membership has been a key to understanding the conflict that has split the country to its foundations. In El Salvador, those displaced by the civil war of the 1980s and early 1990s were mainly peasants. Their plight was described to Deng as a class problem, one of economic disparity. He found this to be true in many respects, and yet he observed that even a cursory look at the physiognomy of the two sides—peasants of indian racial stock on the one and governments and landowners of European or mixed ancestry on the other—was enough to show the issue to be more complicated than simple differences in economic or class standing. The same was true of Colombia and Peru, two other Latin American countries Deng visited, where indigenous populations were both the poorest and the most affected by internal displacement.

But as both Deng and UN Secretary-General Kofi Annan have emphasized, race, language, religion, or culture are not in themselves the cause of conflict. Deng has pointed out that "it is never the mere differences of identity based on ethnic grounds that generate conflict, but the consequences of those differences in sharing power and the related distribution of resources and opportunities. . . . The role of political leadership at all levels, from local to national, is pivotal."[1] And in a 1996 article, "The Peacekeeping Prescription," Annan elaborated, "In societies where they are accepted and respected, people of vastly different backgrounds live peacefully and productively together. Ethnic differences become charged . . . when they are used for political ends."[2] Problems most frequently arise when a dominant group seeks to impose its identity on others or advance its interests over those of others—and when political leaders exploit resentments, prejudices, and passions in their attempt to gain or retain a hold on power.

Over the past decade crises of national identity have been one of the main causes of internal displacement. They have engen-

---

1. Roberta Cohen and Francis Deng, *Masses in Flight: The Global Crisis of Internal Displacement* (Brookings, 1998), p. 21.

2. Kofi Annan, "The Peacekeeping Prescription," in *Preventive Diplomacy*, edited by Kevin M. Cahill (Basic Books, 1996), p. 176.

**The only shelter available to these internally displaced Bosnian women and children in 1994 was a former chicken breeding building in Turanj, Bosnia.**

Photograph by Sebastiao Salgado.

dered massive violations of fundamental human rights and freedoms, grave compromises of economic and social development, breakdowns of civil order, and attempts at "ethnic cleansing" and even genocide.

But simply to call the victims of these crises internally displaced is to apply to them a label so impersonal as to strip them of their essential humanity, to make them little more than a bureaucratic category. To understand the problem of internal displacement we need first of all to take a closer look at just who are the internally displaced.

# Who Are the Internally Displaced?

Defining a thing or a problem sometimes is the hardest part of dealing with it. We may be confident that we know it when we see it but still have trouble fitting it into so many words.

That is the predicament in which the international community finds itself with regard to internal displacement. It has no universally agreed definition for those internally displaced who should be considered to be in need of assistance and protection by the international community. There is a widely used working definition set out in a UN Commission on Human Rights report issued in 1992 by Secretary-General Boutros-Ghali. It calls the internally displaced

> Persons who have been forced to flee their homes suddenly or unexpectedly in large numbers, as a result of armed conflict, internal strife, systematic violations of human rights or natural or man-made disasters, and who are within the territory of their own country.[1]

---

1. Commission on Human Rights, *Analytical Report of the Secretary-General on Internally Displaced Persons,* E/CN,4/1992/23 (United Nations, February 14, 1992), para. 17.

Good enough, one might say. It covers the two central elements: coerced movement and remaining within one's national borders. Few would disagree that persons forced from their homes by armed conflict, internal strife, and systematic abuses of human rights and freedoms warrant the sympathetic attention of the international community. After all, that and more is given to those who escape the borders of their country—to refugees. Why should it be denied to those caught within the borders of their country?

But what of persons uprooted by natural disasters? Victims of flood, earthquake, cyclone, drought, or nuclear or chemical disaster would not qualify as refugees if they crossed a border. In most cases such persons are helped by their governments; or if their governments lack the resources, others voluntarily chip in. But if disaster is accompanied by severe neglect or abuses of human, political, or civil rights, should the international community not assume some responsibility for its victims? On those grounds the working definition rightly encompasses them.

In other respects, however, the working definition may seem too narrow. Limiting the internally displaced to those forced to flee their homes "suddenly and unexpectedly in large numbers" excludes some of the most serious cases. Bosnian Muslims did not flee their homes in Banja Luka and other areas; they were expelled. In Burma under the military junta, in Iraq under Saddam Hussein's rule, and in Ethiopia under the Mengistu dictatorship, hundreds of thousands were forcibly moved, at times with considerable advance notice. In Colombia, a country with a huge continuing problem of internal displacement, people often flee in small numbers in the hope of making themselves inconspicuous. The working definition would cover none of these.

As part of his mandate as the representative of the secretary-general on internally displaced persons, Francis Deng has sought to refine the UN working definition to take account of these shortcomings. In consultation with international lawyers and

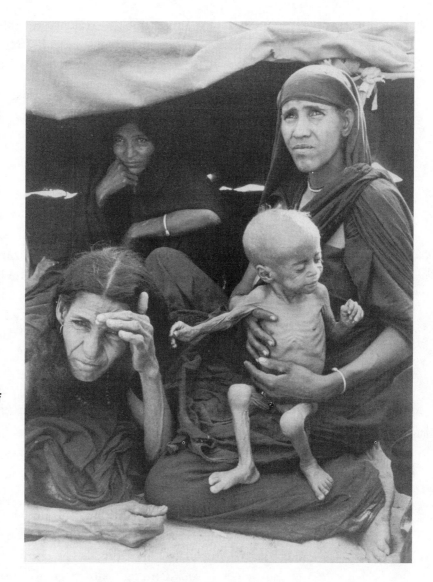

**Severe drought in West Africa's Sahel region forced tens of thousands of nomadic cattle herders into camps such as the one in Lazaret, Niger.**

Photograph by
W. van de Linde,
Office of the UN High
Commissioner for
Refugees.

other experts, he developed a broader definition of the internally displaced as persons or groups of persons

> who have been forced or obliged to flee or to leave their homes or places of habitual residence in particular as a result of, or in order to avoid the effects of, armed conflict,

situations of generalized violence, violations of human rights or natural or human-made disasters, and who have not crossed an internationally recognized state border.

This definition is written to include those forced out as well as those who flee or leave. It retains a category of natural and man-made disasters, and by use of the words "in particular" signals that it does not intend arbitrarily to exclude any serious future situation.

Looking behind the legal language, who in fact are the internally displaced? The facts and figures that would make it possible to answer the question in absolute detail are lacking. The United Nations is still in the initial stages of organizing systematic collection of data on the internally displaced. The U.S. Committee for Refugees, a nongovernmental organization, has gathered statistics on the internally displaced for over a decade; and the Norwegian Refugee Council in its Global Survey of Internally Displaced People, issued in 1998, has also published figures on internal displacement. Both, however, recognize that obtaining accurate data is a very difficult task even under the best of circumstances.

Still, some general observations can be made. First, while internal displacement knows no racial or class boundaries, it is overwhelmingly the lot of the world's poor. In ethnic conflicts in particular, it is possible to find among the displaced both rural and urban dwellers as well as persons of widely varying economic status and educational background. This notwithstanding, by far the largest single element is the rural poor. In Sudan most of the internally displaced are from the predominantly rural south; in Turkey the overwhelming majority are Kurdish villagers from the country's southeastern region; in Latin America they are mostly poor rural, indigenous people, often non-Spanish speaking.

A second and no less important observation is that the overwhelming majority of the internally displaced are women and their dependent children. With most instances of displacement

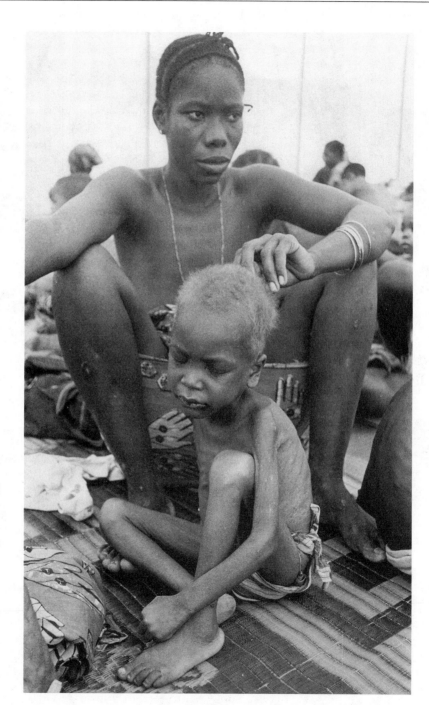

**This child, emaciated and turned gray from starvation, was among the hundreds of thousands displaced by civil war in Liberia and Sierra Leone during the early 1990s.**

Photograph by L. Taylor, Office of the UN High Commissioner for Refugees.

**Forced displacement can be as destructive of the environment as of people's lives, as is illustrated by this camp for internally displaced persons at Kibeho in Rwanda in 1994.**

Photograph by
A. Hollmann,
Office of the UN High
Commissioner for
Refugees.

due to civil war, men either join or are drafted into the fighting ranks of one side or another, are killed or disabled, or flee to avoid recruitment. Women are left as heads of households, but are both defenseless and without resources in a violent setting. Instances of displaced women being raped are common; and at times they have found no recourse but to resort to prostitution to feed themselves and their children.

Children suffer the most. Child malnutrition rates as high as 70 percent have been recorded in some mass displacements. Children living in displaced persons camps usually do not have access either to adequate health care or education. Often they are separated from their families. In Africa, in particular, children have been forcibly conscripted into the fighting ranks of one side or another; and in addition to participating in killings they have been subjected to serious abuse. In Mozambique during the civil war of the 1980s, rebel troops forced children to serve as porters, sexual partners, and human shields; much the same happened in Liberia during the civil war of the 1990s.

Displacement often is thought of as a temporary problem, one that will disappear with the return or resettlement of the displaced. But some mass displacements have persisted for decades and have not been fully resolved even with the passage from one generation to another. Return, in particular, is a more complicated enterprise than is generally understood. Conditions of insecurity may last for years. When the displaced do seek to return, they may find their land and their homes occupied by others or sometimes in the possession of a hostile ethnic group or under the control of a hostile country. Resettlement, which has its own particular difficulties and complications, may be the only practical solution.

Prolonged displacement often leads to widespread loss of skills. Craftsmen lose or sell their tools and find no use for their skills in new areas with limited markets. Farmers are slower to lose skills, but separation from the land affects every aspect of their and their families' existence.

And the displaced are by no means the only ones affected. Sometimes the extent of displacement has been so great that one could speak, as in the case of Liberia, of whole societies becoming displaced. Of the countries with major conflicts since 1980, ten had more than 40 percent of their population displaced, with cataclysmic consequences for the population as a whole. Displacement in fact can be said to have a multiplier effect. As a community loses population it also loses skills, and both its economic and its social equilibrium are affected. Sometimes entire communities or regions have become depopulated. Neglected agricultural land becomes uncultivable. Uncared for trees cease to bear fruit and wither. Homes and other buildings deteriorate.

When the displaced flee in large numbers to rural areas they inevitably wreak havoc with the environment, polluting streams and groundwater sources and stripping forests and grasslands for fuel. In Rwanda, internally displaced persons and returning refugees have done grevious damage to national parks and forests that once were an important source of foreign exchange earnings from tourism. When the internally displaced flee to urban centers, as they have in large numbers in Africa and Latin America, the result is overcrowding, sometimes the doubling or tripling of a city's population. Often the only shelter they find is in shanty-towns on the outskirts of major cities, without access to sanitation, clean running water, and medical, educational, or other services and with few possibilities for employment.

Even if they were not poor before fleeing or being driven from their homes, the internally displaced quickly become the poorest of the poor, subject to abuse and exploitation and to rates of malnutrition, disease, and mortality well beyond those of the still settled population.

# Chapter Three

# The Internally Displaced: Where and Why?

**Rebels found me and took me to their camp. Then they sent for my children, saying, "see what we are going to do to your father." They held my arms down against a log and then cut them off. Then they let us go. Some soldiers found me on the road and brought me here to the hospital.**

U.S. Committee for Refugees, "The Usual People, Refugees and Internally Displaced Persons from Sierra Leone," Issue Brief, February 1995

N o continent has been spared the scourge of internal displacement or the cruelty that is often associated with it, but one has suffered more grievously than others: Africa. Some 10 million persons are internally displaced in Africa today, nearly all in the continent's sub-Saharan region.

The list of African countries with large numbers of internally displaced reads like the roster of the continent's many civil wars. Far and away the worst case—in Africa or anywhere else in the world—is Sudan, with four million internally displaced persons. Virtually all are southern Sudanese driven from their homes by the civil war that has afflicted the country periodically since it became independent in 1956. Next, in approximate order of magnitude, come Angola, Liberia, and Sierra Leone. Angola's civil war inflicted such disaster that more than a million persons remained internally displaced there over two years after a peace agreement was reached. The civil war in Liberia that began in 1990 at one time or another uprooted virtually the entire two and one-half million people of the country. In 1997, after elections had been held and the country appeared to be heading into a period of stability, a million Liberians remained internally displaced. Sierra Leone's civil war was a spillover from that in Liberia. It made a million or more displaced from their homes yet still within the borders of their country.

**Sudan's civil war, the longest running in Africa, has displaced millions and inflicted untold misery. As usual, children have suffered the most.**

Photograph by Roger P. Winter, U.S. Committee for Refugees.

Settlement of the civil war in Mozambique reduced the number of internally displaced from 3 million in 1993 to 500,000 by mid-1996. This was a monumental achievement, made possible by close and effective collaboration between the national government and international humanitarian and nongovernmental organizations. Other civil wars, some ongoing and others settled, have left hundreds of thousands internally displaced in Rwanda, Burundi, Ethiopia, and Somalia, while political repression in Kenya and the Congo (formerly Zaire) has caused hundreds of thousands more to be uprooted. In a distinct category, 500,000 black South Africans remain internally displaced, the legacy of the policies of that country's now defunct apartheid regime.

The reader might well ask why Africa should have become afflicted by so many civil wars driving such large numbers of people from their homes. One cause has been examined already: crises of national identity, often manipulated by governments and by opposition groups. The European great powers that divided Africa among themselves in the nineteenth century drew borders for their own convenience. These rarely if ever took cognizance of African ethnic, linguistic, or tribal realities. The leaders of newly independent African states of the second half of the twentieth century were left with the herculean task of infusing a sense of national unity into a hodgepodge of diverse, competing, and sometimes warring linguistic, tribal, and clan groups. Many did not even try; those few who did have yet to succeed in any substantial measure.

The dividing lines among Africans have been deepened by intense poverty and fierce competition for scarce resources. Most of the countries that have been mentioned are among the world's thirty poorest. Rwanda and Burundi, where recurrent bouts of killing between Hutus and Tutsis have created hundreds of thousands of internally displaced, have the distinction of being among the world's most heavily populated countries as well as among its

**In southern Sudan at an encampment for the internally displaced.**

Photograph by Roger P. Winter, U.S. Committee for Refugees.

poorest. Pressure on the land is intense. Competition for control of resources has been a major element in the civil wars in Liberia and Sierra Leone and a factor of no small significance in other conflicts. The conflict in Sudan, in appearance mainly a matter of north versus south and Muslims versus Christians and Animists, is also about political and economic power. As Hiram Ruiz has written in his case study on Sudan in the second volume of Roberta Cohen and Francis Deng's study on internal displacement, *The Forsaken People*, "elite northerners have dominated the Sudan politically and economically since independence and continue to covet the south's natural resources."

Although Africa was on the margins of post–World War II competition between the United States and the Soviet Union, several of its most disruptive conflicts can be traced in substantial part to the cold war. The two superpowers enlisted client governments and political or opposition movements and supplied them with arms that enabled them to establish control over a state or pursue a war against an insurgency or an opposing state. With Soviet arms, Somalia invaded Ethiopia in 1978; and with Soviet arms and assistance, Ethiopia repelled the Somali invasion and for more than a decade thereafter waged an ultimately vain war to suppress Eritrea's drive for independence. In Mozambique and Angola the Soviet Union supplied arms to ideologically allied regimes to beat back insurgencies supported in Angola by the United States and in Mozambique by minority white governments in neighboring Rhodesia and South Africa. In Liberia, Somalia, and Zaire, U.S. arms deliveries during the 1980s were critical in keeping corrupt and repressive regimes in power long beyond their time. The withdrawal of U.S. assistance at the end of the cold war brought the collapse of these regimes, with consequences made all the more disastrous by their artificially prolonged existence. It is no coincidence that the African states that were most closely aligned with and received the highest levels of aid from the two cold war protagonists were those that experienced, then or later, the most extreme violence and the greatest killing, destruction of property, and internal displacement.

Europe, broadly defined to include Turkey and the Caucasus region of the former Soviet Union, counted approximately 5 million internally displaced in 1997. "Waves of ethnic dislocation" is how Cohen and Deng characterize Europe's internally displaced in *Masses in Flight*. Ethnic conflict attendant upon the collapse of communist regimes in the late 1980s and early 1990s accounts for slightly more than half the 5 million. Authoritarian communism was the glue that held diverse and often mutually antagonistic ethnic communities together. When its hold crumbled, age-old rivalries, competition for territory, and incitement by opportunistic political leaders plunged the former Yugoslavia and the Caucasus region of the former Soviet Union into war. In Bosnia and Croatia, despite NATO's intervention at the end of 1995, its continuing military presence, and the various measures taken to settle the conflict among Serbs, Muslims, and Croats, 1.2 million people remain internally displaced: 1 million in Bosnia and Herzegovina and more than 200,000 in Croatia. Fighting in the Serbian province of Kosovo between Serb forces and ethnic Albanian rebels displaced up to 300,000 more persons internally during 1998. The wars in Chechnya between Chechen separatists and Russian forces, in the Caucasus between Armenians and Azerbaijanis, and in Georgia, have left more than 1 million others uprooted long after fighting ceased.

Ethnic conflict in Turkey and Cyprus accounts for most of the rest of Europe's 5 million displaced. The conflicts between Turks and Kurds in Turkey proper and between Turkish and Greek Cypriots are long-standing and independent of the cold war or the collapse of communist regimes. Some 2 million Kurds are currently estimated to be internally displaced in Turkey, mostly rural people driven from their homes in southeastern Turkey as a result of fighting between government forces and a long-running

**Krajina Serbs in August 1995, on the road between the frontier post of Badovinci and the town of Sabac, fled carrying with them only bare essentials. Until the civil war in the former Yugoslavia, Serbs were the majority in the Krajina; today almost none remain in the region.**

Photograph by Sebastiao Salgado.

Kurdish insurgency. In Cyprus more than a quarter of a million Greek Cypriots remain displaced since Turkey's 1974 invasion of the island.

In Asia—broadly defined to run from the shores of the eastern Mediterranean to the western rim of the Pacific ocean—internal displacement has been mainly limited to a patchwork of countries strewn across the continent's western, central, southern, and southeastern regions. The numbers, 5 million altogether, are small relative to Asia's overall population. But many of the countries that have had problems with displacement—Lebanon, Iraq, Tajikistan, Afghanistan, India, Sri Lanka, Burma, Cambodia, and the Philippines—have had them in particularly virulent form.

Unlike Europe, in Asia ethnic conflict was only one of several causes of conflict. The civil war in Lebanon offers an example. It pitted Christian, Muslim, and Druze factions against one another but was made infinitely worse by the broader and more deeply political dispute between Israelis, Palestinians, and Syrians who made Lebanon into a proxy battleground. At its height the Lebanese civil war forced approximately 1 million persons from their homes. Although significant fighting among Lebanese factions came to an end in 1990, nearly half a million Lebanese remain internally displaced, the majority in the Christian Mount Lebanon region.

The large numbers of internally and externally displaced persons produced by Iraq since its defeat in the Gulf War in February 1991 are the work of a vicious government seeking ruthlessly to reassert control over ethnic communities eager to escape its dominance. The most massive displacement took place in Iraq in the spring of 1991 as 2 million Kurds fled their homes desperately seeking safety from Saddam Hussein's army in the country's northern mountain fastness or across the borders in Turkey and Iran. In southern Iraq, hundreds of thousands fled into the marshlands or across the border into Iran after Saddam's army suppressed a Shiite Muslim rebellion. Currently 650,000 remain displaced in the Kurdish zone. In the south the number of internally displaced is impossible to estimate with any accuracy. The Iraqi regime has drained the marshlands and waged a cruel war against their inhabitants. But it has cast such a thick shroud of secrecy over its operations there that only wild guesses can be made at the numbers of displaced and at-risk persons—somewhere between 40,000 and 1 million.

The small, poor, and remote central Asian republic of Tajikistan plunged into civil war when it became independent in 1991 following the breakup of the Soviet Union. The fighting made an estimated 600,000 people, a tenth of the country's population, internally displaced and sent tens of thousands fleeing into neighboring Afghanistan. Regional rivalries played as important a role as did conflict between competing ethnic and clan groups.

**Civil war in newly independent Tajikistan uprooted 600,000 from their homes. These Tajik children, living in a war-damaged village near Dushanbe, were among the victims.**

Photograph by Jennifer McLean Marsh, Brookings Institution.

Cold war politics was the direct cause of the havoc wreaked in Afghanistan and Cambodia. Millions of Afghans became uprooted, both as refugees and as internally displaced, during the years of Soviet occupation as Soviet troops battled Mujahedin guerrilla fighters backed by the United States, Pakistan, and Saudi Arabia. Many returned home after the Soviet-backed Afghan government fell, but half a million were estimated to remain displaced at the end of 1995. Intense fighting that resumed in 1996 caused many thousands of others to become displaced.

Cambodia's fragile equilibrium was destroyed by the Vietnam War and U.S. intervention. The Pol Pot regime, which defeated a U.S.-backed government in 1975, killed more than a million persons and forcibly uprooted almost all the rest of the country's population. It was Vietnam, paradoxically, that first came to the rescue, easing but not resolving Cambodia's plight through its invasion in 1978. Since the Vietnamese withdrawal in the late 1980s, hundreds of thousands of Cambodian refugees and internally displaced persons have been repatriated and resettled under UN programs. Nonetheless, land mines and sporadic fighting among Cambodian factions have caused a floating population of some 50,000 to remain displaced.

Ethnic conflict is at the heart of the civil war that has raged in Sri Lanka during the past decade and a half. British rule favored the Tamil minority. After Britain left, the policies of the Sinhalese majority governments in the 1970s and 1980s persuaded Tamils that they were in danger of being reduced to secondary status. Fighting between the Sri Lankan army and security forces and the Liberation Tigers of Tamil Eelam (LTTE) has caused more than 1 million persons out of a total population of 17 million to become displaced from their homes. The Sri Lankan government is one of the few to issue reliable statistics on its internally displaced population. It reported 570,453 internally displaced at the end of September 1995. A military operation launched at the end of 1995 is believed to have displaced 400,000 more, bringing the most recent estimate of internally displaced in Sri Lanka to some 900,000.

India is estimated to have 250,000 persons internally displaced by the conflict between the government and Muslim separatists in Kashmir. In Burma (officially renamed Myanmar) the military junta's repression of minority ethnic groups and political opponents is estimated to have created between 500,000 and 1 million internally displaced persons. Reliable figures are unavailable because the junta bars access by international human rights and humanitarian organizations. However, large numbers of displaced persons are reported to have been forcibly recruited by the

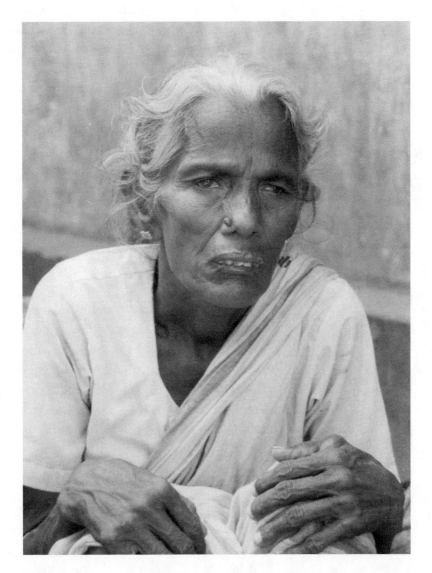

**This woman, one of hundreds of thousands of Sri Lankans displaced by fighting between government forces and Tamil separatists in late 1995 and 1996, sought refuge in an abandoned public building.**

Photograph by Hiram Ruiz, U.S. Committee for Refugees.

government as labor for road and other construction projects. In the Philippines, insurgencies primarily in the southern islands have caused tens of thousands to become internally displaced.

In Latin America, cold war rivalries, authoritarian regimes, and conflict between European or elites of mixed-race origin and indigenous majorities, especially over land distribution, caused severe crises of internal displacement during the 1980s and early 1990s. The civil war in El Salvador alone uprooted approximately 1 million persons; hundreds of thousands of others were displaced in Guatemala and Nicaragua. In Haiti, abuses perpetrated during the military rule following the ouster of President Aristide displaced several hundred thousand persons within the country and generated an outpouring of refugees.

Political settlements have brought significant improvements in Central America and Haiti. By the mid-1990s internal displacement had largely been resolved in El Salvador and Nicaragua, while contradictory figures have been advanced for Haiti. Internal displacement remained a serious problem in Guatemala, Peru, and Colombia.

The origins of the civil war in Guatemala between the government and insurgent guerrillas, mainly impoverished Mayan Indian peasants, date back several decades. Violence by the army against civilians caused large-scale flight. During the worst period, between 1979 and 1983, soldiers were said to have burned more than 440 villages. Women and girls were raped, and men and boys were killed or forceably conscripted into the military. The civil war drew to a close in 1995 and 1996 as a cease-fire and a political settlement negotiated under UN auspices took hold. At that time the number of those displaced was in dispute, with estimates ranging from 200,000 to 1.5 million.

In Peru, rapid population growth after World War II and widespread poverty and government neglect gave rise to two leftist movements of extreme violence, the Sendero Luminoso, or Shining Path, and the Tupac Amaru Revolutionary Movement. Fighting between these groups and government forces during the 1980s caused almost a million persons, most of them Andean villagers of Indian ancestry, to flee their homes. Most went to Lima where they created vast shantytowns on the city's periphery. Since

**Many of the estimated 1 million Peruvians uprooted by the insurgency and equally violent counterinsurgency of the late 1980s and early 1990s sought refuge in cities, where they set up shantytowns such as this one near Lima.**

Photograph by Hiram Ruiz, U.S. Committee for Refugees.

the capture of the Shining Path leadership in 1992, the insurgency has gradually wound down; by the mid-1990s it retained strength only in the remote Amazon region. Under government-sponsored programs, 120,000 to 250,000 internally displaced persons returned home during 1994 and 1995. However, an estimated 600,000 remain displaced.

Although the worst of Peru's problems of internal displacement appears past, Colombia's are on the rise. Colombia currently suffers the most serious case of internal displacement of any country in the Western Hemisphere. In one sense, it offers an extraordinary example of internal displacement as a phenomenon of a society unable to contain a crisis of criminality. Murder was the number one cause of death in Colombia in 1995, the latest

**Eight months after first being displaced, more than a thousand persons in Turbo, Colombia, were still living in the town's former sports hall.**

Photograph by Hiram Ruiz, U.S. Committee for Refugees.

year for which statistics are available. The country had the highest homocide rate in the world: 25,222 reported killings in a population of approximately 36 million. Violence, a government study acknowledged, is the method traditionally used in Colombia for conflict resolution.

By another measure, however, Colombia's problem is simply one of the collapse of state authority. Leftist guerrillas and private armies run by large landowners and drug barons and often backed by the Colombian army control half the country. Even in the part under government control the power of the state and the rule of law are much diminished. In the overarching atmosphere of violence engendered by this conflict, internal displacement became the mode of escape chosen by more than a million persons between 1985 and 1997. Current estimates put the number of internally displaced at between 600,000 and 1 million. Two-thirds are rural people; many have been chased from their land by drug cartels looking to expand their acreage of crop cultivation or by wealthy cattle ranchers or other powerful economic interests. Others targeted are persons of left-leaning views, members of the Catholic clergy or others who work with the poor and the displaced, and anyone who may have become involved in a personal vendetta. Violence and internal displacement have been on the increase since 1992 when both left and right wing paramilitary groups stepped up their operations.

With this brief survey there has been established in broad outline where most of the world's 20 million to 25 million internally displaced are and why they became displaced. Let us turn now to look at what is being done to help them.

*Chapter Four*

# Who Helps the Internally Displaced?

**My name is Milana. I am 16 and I am an internally displaced person. I had never heard of internally displaced persons before December 1994 when I fled Grozny.**

From "An Interrupted Life," *Refugees* magazine, no. 107, 1997

When fighting started in the Chechen capital, Milana's father sent her with neighbors to a safe village. When the fighting engulfed the village as well, she fled, alone. She was taken in by a family, then transferred to a center run by the UN High Commissioner for Refugees where she was given shelter and new clothes and shoes, and receives a special monthly distribution of food. She has lost contact with her parents and her education has been disrupted, perhaps irremediably. But she has hope. "I think that I might be alright," she says.

Others are not so fortunate. Most internally displaced find themselves without adequate shelter, food, medical care, and sanitation and with little or no protection from abuse by governments or insurgent groups.

Today most UN and other major international humanitarian organizations take some part in assisting and protecting the internally displaced even though none has a specific, legally recognized mandate to do so. This chapter looks at who the main ones are and just what they are doing.

# The UN Agencies

Since World War II an array of UN agencies has been established to assist refugees and women and children; address emergency situations, food provision, and medical needs; and promote development. Most are of long standing: the UN High Commissioner for Refugees (UNHCR), the UN Development Programme (UNDP), the World Food Programme (WFP), the UN Children's Fund (UNICEF), and the World Health Organization (WHO). An important new one has recently been added to the list: the Office of the High Commissioner for Human Rights.

### United Nations High Commissioner for Refugees

Of all the UN agencies UNHCR is the one that has taken on the broadest overall responsibility for helping the internally displaced, even though its statute gives it no mandate for doing so. At times it has intervened at the request of the UN secretary-general and the General Assembly to assist and protect the internally displaced, most notably and extensively in the former Yugoslavia.

In other instances UNHCR has acted under authorization given by the General Assembly in 1993 to extend its assistance to internally displaced persons when both refugees and internally displaced persons are so intertwined that it would be impossible or inadvisable to help one group and not the other. On that basis the agency has worked with the internally displaced in Guatemala, Sierra Leone, Angola, and Azerbaijan, where the displaced were mixed with returning refugees. In Tajikistan it assumed an even broader role not directly linked to returning refugees. But in other countries it has taken little or no part in aiding the internally displaced, even when, as in Colombia, a government has asked it to do so.

By virtue of its long and successful experience in protecting and assisting refugees, UNHCR is generally considered to be the best-equipped of UN agencies to take on similar responsibilities for internally displaced persons. But venturing into protecting and assisting the internally displaced has been a challenge that the agency has assumed with both hesitation and frequent misgivings. Refugees are by definition outside the borders of their country. UNHCR has an internationally recognized legal mandate to protect and assist them. For the internally displaced it has nothing of the kind; its operations are circumscribed by what the host government will tolerate, and they involve higher risks to agency staff. Some in UNHCR are known to fear that greater involvement with the internally displaced will change the character of the organization and distract it from its primary responsibility. In Sudan, the country with the largest number of internally displaced persons (about 4 million), it has declined to operate programs for them, evidently for fear that doing so would damage its relations with the Sudanese government and impair its ability to assist and protect refugees in that country. Refugee advocates have expressed concern that by assisting and protecting internally displaced persons the agency may put itself in the position of discouraging persons in danger from becoming refugees, and that its actions in that sense could offer governments a pretext for refusal to grant asylum.

In 1997 UNHCR deemed 4.8 million internally displaced persons to be "of concern" to it. The figure, small in comparison to the overall need, nonetheless represents a broadening of the agency's scope of activities for the internally displaced.

### United Nations Development Programme

As its name implies the UN Development Programme is an economic development agency. It long conceived of itself as being

**In Azerbaijan, so many school buildings were taken to shelter the internally displaced that the UNHCR set up this tent school, and many others like it, both for displaced and for local children.**

Photograph by
R. Redmond,
Office of the UN High
Commissioner for
Refugees.

exclusively developmental, shunning involvement in assistance or protection in emergency situations. In recent years, however, it has been brought into dealing with the internally displaced, largely because in most cases UNDP resident representatives serve as resident coordinators for the entire UN system in a country. In 1990 the General Assembly assigned resident coordinators "the function of coordinating assistance to the internally displaced, in close cooperation with governments, local representatives of donor countries and the United Nations agencies in the field."[1]

---

1. General Assembly, Resolution 44/136 (United Nations, February 27, 1990).

The transition to a broader function has not been without its discomforts. Within the agency itself some have questioned the wisdom of assuming responsibilities beyond development. UNDP resident representatives have at times lacked both experience and interest in matters beyond their developmental mandate. Most have not considered human rights and protection activities to be compatible with their work as UNDP resident representatives; and often they have been uncomfortable dealing with issues that may involve tension with host government authorities. Fear of damaging relations with the host government has kept some representatives from raising protection issues or even acknowledging serious problems of internal displacement in their country of assignment.

Nonetheless, both at the headquarters and in the field the agency has moved to adapt itself to the new circumstances. In 1990 it endorsed the view that relief and development work should be more closely linked and that UNDP staff should engage themselves more fully in the early phases of emergencies. An emergency division has been created within the agency, and training courses in disaster management have been set up for resident representatives. Still, because the representatives have not always been well suited to act as coordinators in emergency situations, the UN's emergency relief coordinator has been authorized to select, in consultation with UNDP and others, a humanitarian coordinator from agencies other than UNDP to act as resident/ humanitarian coordinator.

In Bosnia-Herzegovina, Cambodia, Central America, and the Horn of Africa, UNDP has undertaken programs to help reintegrate uprooted persons. It has declared internally displaced persons to be "the largest specific target group" of agency programs in countries in postcrisis circumstances. In 1995 the agency set aside 5 percent of its core resources ($50 million) for development activities in countries in emergency situations.

**World Food Programme**

The World Food Programme, headquartered in Rome, is the single largest provider of food to the internally displaced. In 1995 it distributed some 2.8 million tons to 14 million internally displaced persons worldwide.

In the past WFP's primary focus was development assistance. In recent years the focus has shifted to refugee and emergency work. These currently account for 70 percent of the agency's $1.5 billion annual budget. Under Executive Director Catherine Bertini, the program has worked to improve its handling of emergency situations. It has created rapid response teams, seconded officers from nongovernmental organizations, organized standby arrangements, stockpiled food and equipment, and moved to increase its oversight of food distribution systems set up through governments and nongovernmental organizations. In the course of the changeover, however, some difficult problems of balance have arisen. The shift to emergency work has at times led to reductions in development programs needed for an integrated approach to dealing with internal displacement. And WFP has been criticized, in its efforts to reduce dependency, for withdrawing food assistance too quickly in some circumstances, leaving needy populations without adequate alternative means.

One problem in particular that the agency has had to address has been discrimination against women in the distribution of food to the internally displaced and other at-risk populations. In the past in camp situations food distribution was generally left in the hands of committees of men drawn from the camp population, despite the fact that the great majority of almost all camp populations are women. The result was that women often received less than their fair share of food and at times have had little choice but to trade sexual favors for food. To correct this, the program directed that there should be "full involvement of women in planning and managing relief assistance" and that distribution of relief food should be made "direct to households, especially women."[2] It will, however, need carefully to monitor individual situations to ensure that the policy is actually carried out.

In most cases WFP itself has not taken the lead in humanitarian emergencies; it has provided food for a program handled by a lead agency or by the coordinated response of several agencies. This it did in the former Yugoslavia, the former Soviet Union, Somalia, and the Great Lakes region of Africa. But the agency has taken the lead in emergency situations in Angola, Cambodia, Liberia, Mozambique, and Sierra Leone.

In its 1996 response to the Economic and Social Council, WFP also formally recognized the higher priority it was already giving to problems of internal displacement by listing as one of its major functions in emergencies to "monitor and report on food distributions to the internally displaced."[3]

## United Nations Children's Fund (UNICEF)

UNICEF is primarily a development organization. As such, traditionally it has preferred to avoid becoming involved in what it calls "loud emergencies," those caused by violence and famine. But the fact that 70 to 90 percent of internally displaced persons are women and their dependent children makes it impossible for the agency to stand aside from emergency situations. After a period of hesitation, recently it has seen its way clear to becoming more actively involved in programs of assistance to the internally displaced.

---

2. World Food Programme, "WFP Response to ECOSOC Resolution 1995/56," reports to the Economic and Social Council, WFP/EB.A/96/7 (United Nations, April 9, 1996), p. 5.

3. World Food Programme, "WFP Response to ECOSOC Resolution 1995/56," p. 5.

**Internally displaced children living in a shantytown on hills above Medellin, Colombia.**

Photograph by Hiram Ruiz, U.S. Committee for Refugees.

Emergency situations now account for just over one-quarter of UNICEF's activities. It has created rapid response teams, stockpiled essential supplies, and made standby arrangements with nongovernmental organizations. A memorandum of agreement signed in 1995 between UNICEF and UNHCR in regard to refugees, returnees, and the internally displaced gives UNICEF responsibility for unaccompanied children within their countries of origin; and the UN Convention on the Rights of the Child gives UNICEF increased authority in the protection of children. Accordingly, the agency has begun to pay more attention to protecting internally displaced children. It has adopted a policy on the protection of children in "especially difficult circumstances" and in various countries has been in the forefront of negotiations to gain access to children in conflict situations. In southern Sudan UNICEF officials have made representations on the forcible conscription of children. In Burundi the agency has helped trace the families of unaccompanied children and has placed more than 10,000 uprooted children with foster families.

In 1995 UNICEF called for measures to protect women and girls from sexual violence, raise the minimum age for military recruitment to 18 years, set up protective "zones of peace" for children, ban the production of antipersonnel land mines, and address the psychosocial rehabilitation of war-damaged children. The challenge for UNICEF will be to ensure that the many laudable changes ordered at headquarters are actually implemented in the field, where the agency has been urged to do far more in providing protection.

## World Health Organization

WHO's traditional role has been to provide technical assistance on health-related matters to state authorities. In emergencies it views its primary task as giving technical guidance to health authorities, the United Nations, and nongovernmental organizations. Unlike most of the other agencies, it does not ordinarily engage in hands-on operational emergency responses involving large numbers of field staff.

Nonetheless, in recent years WHO has moved toward a more active role in humanitarian emergencies. Its executive board and the World Health Assembly have approved the agency's carrying out limited operational activities. In Rwanda the agency joined in efforts to aid refugees and internally displaced persons. It has also carried out emergency work in the former Yugoslavia, Afghanistan, Tajikistan, and Iraq. In 1995 the agency announced that it would assume a more active role in defense of the victims of armed conflict.

These changes notwithstanding, death rates among internally displaced populations are among the highest of all groups in humanitarian emergencies, and they are often caused by inattention to clean water, sanitation, and timely immunizations. In Somalia, for example, in the early 1990s most deaths were attributed not to starvation but to insufficient attention to public health. Clearly, there is scope for further expansion of WHO's activities in situations of internal displacement.

## Office of the High Commissioner for Human Rights

The position of high commissioner was established in 1994 with the rank of under-secretary-general and a broad mandate to promote and protect human rights. The first high commissioner, José Aya la Lasso, began developing a capacity to carry out meaningful operational activities in humanitarian emergencies. He strengthened the office's rapid response mechanisms and created a roster of human rights staff who could be sent to the field on short notice, working with other UN agencies as well as regional and nongovernmental organizations. In Rwanda in 1995 he deployed more than 130 human rights field staff to help safeguard the return of the internally displaced.

The Office of the High Commissioner for Human Rights has the potential to play an important role in protecting populations at risk. Thus far, however, limited resources and staff have seriously constrained its initiatives. High Commissioner Mary Robinson, appointed in the fall of 1997, has expressed her intention to strengthen the operational capacity of her office in emergency situations. Among the challenges she faces will be to ensure that recommendations regarding internally displaced persons made by representatives and rapporteurs of the Commission on Human Rights are carried out. To do so, she will have to be willing to engage in vigorous private and public diplomacy.

## Outside the UN Framework

Two other organizations with worldwide reaches comparable to UN agencies also contribute to the protection and assistance of the internally displaced: the International Committee of the Red Cross (ICRC) and the International Organization for Migration (IOM).

### International Committee of the Red Cross

Although ICRC is a private organization founded and run outside the UN framework, with its staff of about 7,000 and an annual budget of $600 million, it operates on the worldwide scale of UN agencies. The organization has the further distinction of holding sole statutory authority under the Geneva Conventions and Protocols for protecting and assisting victims of both international and noninternational conflicts. This gives it a clear mandate to intervene on behalf of persons internally displaced by civil wars, the main cause of internal displacement in the post–cold war era. In recent years it has devoted more than 80 percent of its budget to protecting and assisting civilians caught up in internal conflicts.

Unlike most UN humanitarian agencies, ICRC considers protection to be as much a part of its responsibilities as assistance. Its representatives extend protection on all sides in conflict situations and seek to reach those whom other humanitarian organizations cannot reach because of hazardous conditions or political obstacles. In Somalia in 1990 and 1991, when UN agencies withdrew owing to dangerous conditions, ICRC stayed on and assumed responsibility for delivering relief supplies. Its statutory authority under the Geneva Conventions and the fact that it is not a part of the UN system give it greater freedom to challenge abusive or recalcitrant governments.

**An ICRC representative meets with Iraqi Kurds internally displaced by Iraqi government military action against the Kurdish district, April 1991.**

Photograph by
Philippe Dutoit,
International Committee
of the Red Cross.

But there are limits to what can be expected of the organization. Its mandate under the Geneva Conventions extends only to situations of international or civil war, not to lesser conflicts that would not qualify as civil wars. Moreover, not all states have ratified the Geneva Conventions and their additional Protocols, and even some that have do not allow ICRC entry or admit that a non-international conflict is taking place on their territory. The organization has been turned away from helping displaced populations by the governments of Guatemala, Turkey, and Burma, all countries that have large numbers of internally displaced.

One of ICRC's strong points is its independence. Its responsibility is to endangered populations, and its vigorous protection has made it one of the most effective of the international agencies dealing with problems of internal displacement. At the same time, its independence has sometimes complicated its ability to work with other agencies in the field. And its policy of keeping violations of humanitarian law confidential has sometimes rankled human rights organizations.

## International Organization for Migration

IOM is an intergovernmental agency not affiliated with the United Nations. Its aim, as its name implies, is to help persons in need of migration assistance, whether internally displaced or refugees. It organizes transport, evacuations, and returns and provides temporary shelter and other material relief. In recent years it has begun also to help in the reintegration of the displaced. In Mozambique it moved more than 100,000 internally displaced persons and returning refugees to their places of origin or choice and provided reintegration assistance. In Angola it has begun to assist in the return and reintegration of some 600,000 internally displaced persons.

IOM seeks to ensure that movement of persons to whom it provides transport assistance is free and voluntary and that they are enabled to reestablish their lives in dignity and self-respect. Nonetheless, the agency acknowledges that "it is sometimes difficult to evaluate whether a decision to leave a country is voluntary or not, given the pressures or incentives that might play a preponderant role in the decisionmaking process."[4] Nongovernmental organizations have urged IOM to increase safeguards in transporting and registering internally displaced persons.

---

4. Richard Perruchoud, "Return Migration: Observations on the Mandate and Activities of IOM," International Organization for Migration, June 1994.

**Following conclusion of agreements ending the civil war in Guatemala, IOM workers assist in the relocation of internally displaced persons, April 1997.**

Photograph by the International Organization for Migration.

Even though it is not a UN agency, IOM has increasingly come to operate as a member of the UN team in humanitarian emergency situations.

These, then, are the main international organizations dealing with displaced persons. The questions are: How are their efforts coordinated? How are gaps filled and duplication avoided? And is the current system the best possible, or can the United Nations and associated agencies do a better job?

# Chapter Five

# Can the UN Do a Better Job?

**Being a displaced person myself, I feel strongly for the newly displaced people I now work with. I try earnestly to understand their needs, and convey them to UNHCR and the other international agencies that are dealing with the internally displaced in Herat.**

Abdul Qader, Afghan Ministry of Repatriation official, from "A Man Who Makes a Difference," *Refugees* Magazine, no. 107, 1997

A t a meeting in Washington at the Carnegie Endowment for International Peace in May 1997, UN High Commissioner for Refugees Sadako Ogata was asked why the UN system had not been able to do more for the internally displaced. Mrs. Ogata, one of the most able and highly respected figures ever to head the refugee agency, had a ready answer: "The problem is sovereignty."[1]

By definition the internally displaced remain within the borders of their own country, subject to the sovereign authority of their governments. Governments have had few objections to giving the international community authority to act on behalf of foreign nationals who have sought refuge on their territory. But they have been distinctly reluctant to allow similar authority to be extended to their own nationals. Even when the internally displaced escape a government's rule, as in an area under the de facto control of a rebel faction, they continue under international law to be subject to its authority.

---

1. Meeting at Carnegie Endowment for International Peace, May 1, 1997.

As late as the first half of the twentieth century, sovereignty was generally understood to confer on states the unquestioned right to do as they pleased within their internationally recognized borders. Noninterference in the internal affairs of states was a hallowed concept, even if in practice it never prevailed without exception (states that disapproved strongly of what another state was doing always found means to make their disapproval known, the ultimate one being war). State sovereignty was widely proclaimed as the ground rule of international comity. When Hitler's government promulgated laws persecuting Germany's Jewish minority and instituted practices of euthanasia, it violated no then existing international legal instrument. No other state tried to oblige it to stop. However repugnant the German government's actions were considered, they were deemed to be within its rightful authority.

The allied victory in World War II marked the beginning of profound changes in the notion that sovereignty conferred immunity from international scrutiny and censure. The United Nations Charter, the Universal Declaration of Human Rights, the Genocide Convention, and the Covenants on Civil and Political Rights and Economic and Social Rights set standards for state conduct not only internationally but domestically. By affixing their signatures to these documents, states gave up many of their traditional rights of sovereignty. If a state violated the standards flagrantly and repeatedly, it could be called to account before the UN Commission on Human Rights. It could be subjected to international censure and boycott by order of the Security Council or General Assembly, or even to international armed intervention, as Iraq experienced in the spring of 1991 following its massive acts of violence against its Kurdish population.

Such steps, however, have been taken only in extreme situations. International covenants have only put limits on state sovereignty, not abolished it. In most instances these limits are vague, flexible, and open to contest. A powerful government, or one that for whatever reason enjoys strategic support, can block efforts to call it to account (as China and Turkey, to name only two, have done). And even a government that is censured or sanctioned can blatantly ignore or flout the international community's verdict with little serious consequence (Burma and Sudan are cases in point).

As an organization of sovereign states, the United Nations itself can act only insofar as it enjoys the consent and support of its state membership. If a government does not like what an international humanitarian organization is doing or proposes to do on its territory, it can block the activity or expel officials of the organization or (in extremis) the organization itself. Many an international humanitarian agency official has had to reflect on the dangers to comfort and career of placing himself at odds with a host government; more than a few have chosen the safer course.

It is only a minority of governments, however, that invoke sovereignty to block assistance to their internally displaced populations. Most either welcome or tolerate the efforts of the international community to help those uprooted from their homes. Sovereignty aside, the other problem—some might say the more serious one—in devising a response to the global crisis of internal displacement is that of giving effective direction and coordination to the work of the UN's vast but inchoate humanitarian assistance and protection machinery.

The United Nations took its first step toward that end in 1990 when the General Assembly assigned to the resident coordinators of the UN Development Programme the function of coordinating assistance in the field to internally displaced persons. Other steps followed promptly. In 1991, to promote a more rapid and coherent response to all emergency situations, the General Assembly created the post of emergency relief coordinator (ERC). In 1992

**The trauma of war and forced displacement is reflected in the distress of Bosnian Muslim women being taken in 1995 by bus from Kladanj on the frontlines to safety in Zenica, inside central Bosnia.**

Photograph by Sebastiao Salgado.

Secretary-General Boutros Boutros-Ghali set up the Department of Humanitarian Affairs (DHA) to assist the ERC in carrying out his functions. That same year Boutros-Ghali appointed Francis M. Deng as his representative on internally displaced persons. Deng was given a broad mandate. He was authorized to monitor displacement worldwide, undertake fact-finding missions, establish dialogues with governments, coordinate with humanitarian and human rights bodies, make proposals for legal and institutional protection, and publish reports for action by the Commission on Human Rights, the General Assembly, and international organizations.

Also in 1992 the Inter-Agency Standing Committee (IASC), comprising the heads of the major international humanitarian and development agencies, was created to give structure and coordination to the work of UN agencies in emergency situations. In 1994 the IASC designated the ERC as "reference point" for requests for assistance and protection in situations of internal displacement. For working-level coordination, it set up a Task Force on Internally Displaced Persons at the UN's Geneva offices.

## How Effectively Did This Structure Operate?

Crucial to the success of coordinated responses to emergencies were the ERC and the Department of Humanitarian Affairs that he headed. DHA was given an ambitious mandate: it was charged with determining which emergencies required coordination by the United Nations, assigning responsibility to agencies in the field, mobilizing contributions from states, allocating funds, and ensuring that emergency relief operations are conceived and carried out so as to promote rehabilitation and reconstruction. In appearance the ERC had the standing needed to do the job. He held the rank of UN under-secretary-general and the chairmanship of the Inter-Agency Standing Committee.

In the view of many observers both inside and outside the UN system, the record of DHA (which was closed down in 1997) and the early ERCs was mixed. DHA experienced some successes but also fell short of what was expected of it. Despite its having been confirmed as focal point for the internally displaced, the department accorded relatively little attention to them. It did not monitor global displacement. Neither did it develop an information system on internally displaced persons. And it was often hesitant to assign responsibilities to other agencies or to advocate on behalf of the internally displaced in the field.

To be sure, DHA labored under distinct disadvantages. It suffered from frequent turnover of leadership. In the five years following its establishment it had three ERCs at its head. None had time to become deeply familiar with problems of internal displacement and set policy for addressing them. Moreover, the department had limited funding compared with operational agencies and no field operational capacity. The ERC, although formally charged with responsibility for coordinating the work of the various humanitarian agencies, did not outrank the agency heads and had no authority to direct their activities.

DHA's work on internal displacement was also obstructed by bureaucratic rivalries within the department, in particular between the Complex Emergency Division in New York and the Task Force on Internally Displaced Persons in Geneva. Senior DHA officers in New York at times appeared to question whether internal displacement really did belong on the department's agenda. And the Geneva Task Force, while enjoying a broad formal mandate, showed limited effectiveness.

Moreover, the department tended to define the needs of internally displaced persons solely in terms of relief, leaving protection largely neglected. Its mandate gave it no protection responsibilities per se, and its staff were hesitant to venture into protection matters, clearly fearing that to do so would antagonize governments with which the agecy had to deal. Needs assessment missions sent out by the department generally had expertise in food aid, water supply, health and sanitation, and shelter, but not in dealing with the security of displaced populations or human rights issues.

It would nonetheless be unfair to blame on DHA alone the deficiencies in the UN's response to internal displacement. The various agencies themselves must share responsibility. Some abstained from assisting the internally displaced on grounds of mandate. Others had insufficient capacity or experience in work-

**Internally displaced Bosnian Muslim woman reading a list posted at Tuzla Airbase in August 1995 of men of the Bosnian army known to have survived the fall of Srebrenica.**

Photograph by R. LeMoyne, Office of the UN High Commissioner for Refugees.

ing with displaced populations. Still others lacked both the experience and the will to offer protection to those at risk. As a result, the UN's ability to respond to crises of internal displacement has been hobbled. Each problem warrants a brief look.

### Selectivity of Response

Selectivity has been a major shortcoming of the UN humanitarian response system. No UN agency can be counted on to respond with predictability to situations of internal displacement, and there is no international accountability when an agency denies coverage to internally displaced populations. Agencies can pick and choose the situations in which they will become involved in light of their mandates, resources, and interests. In 1996, for example, of the 4.8 million internally displaced persons that UNHCR deemed to be of concern to it, only 1 million were in Africa, a continent with nearly 10 million internally displaced persons. Among those excluded were the approximately 4 million internally displaced in Sudan. In Burundi in 1996 UNICEF decided not to assume responsibility for Tutsi women and children in camps for fear of antagonizing the Hutu population outside. In Colombia, currently the worst case of internal displacement in Latin America, and in Peru, UN agencies have not as yet taken on significant responsibilities despite urgings by the governments of these two countries and by the representative of the secretary-general on internally displaced persons. In Burma, whose government does not acknowledge a problem of internal displacement (independent observers estimate 500,000 to 1 million internally displaced), UN agencies have abstained even from attempting to collect information on forcible displacement. In Turkey no UN agency has sought to challenge that country's refusal of international assistance to the some 2 million Kurds reported to be internally displaced.

## Ineffective Coordination

As one observer is reported to have commented, "Everyone is in favor of coordination, but no one wants to be coordinated." Agencies have tended to go their own way and to act selectively, focusing on their own programs and at times little inclined to subordinate their priorities to overall requirements. DHA's Geneva-based Task Force on Internally Displaced Persons lacked authority to compel coordination but was not even effective in recommending better divisions of labor or pointing out specific situations that agencies had overlooked.

## Inadequate Attention to Protection

Although security is at times even more important for the internally displaced than food, it has been given far less attention. Internally displaced persons in Bosnia received relief supplies, but protection was often weak or nonexistent. A case study on the former Yugoslavia published in Roberta Cohen and Francis Deng's *The Forsaken People* found that "UN personnel acted as if the most, and sometimes the only, essential undertaking was the delivery of relief goods," whereas food itself could be of little use to populations in danger of mass slaughter. In Kibeho, Rwanda, in 1995 thousands were massacred at a camp for internally displaced persons where coordination of relief was carried out effectively by the United Nations but attention to protection was minimal. In Angola and Liberia the World Food Program became the lead UN agency because food and logistics were deemed the most critical needs; equally severe protection problems received less attention.

## Insufficient Reintegration and Development Support

One of the major findings of *Masses in Flight* is that lack of attention to the successful return and rehabilitation of displaced populations can put in jeopardy the entire reconciliation and reintegration process. When internally displaced persons are returned without consideration for their safety or ability to reintegrate, they may find their homes occupied by others and their personal security threatened. In such situations they often become displaced a second time.

As a result, humanitarian agencies have increasingly become involved in monitoring returns and providing reintegration assistance. In Tajikistan, UNHCR closely monitored conditions in areas of concentrated return and worked with local authorities to improve physical security for the displaced; and in Mozambique it and other agencies have provided reintegration support. UNHCR has developed "quick impact projects" to restore roads, schools, and health care facilities and provide income-earning opportunities to returning refugees, internally displaced persons, and local residents. These income-generating efforts, however, need to be linked to longer-term development projects if they are to be self-sustaining. Development agencies often do not incorporate these projects into their plans. Usually they do not have adequate funds for rehabilitation purposes that do not fit into traditional development functions.

## Doing a Better Job

So how can the United Nations organize itself to do a better job of assisting and protecting the internally displaced? What manner of institutional or operational reform would be best calculated to remedy the shortcomings reviewed above? The issue has been a subject of wide-ranging debate both inside and outside the United Nations in recent years. On the institutional side, proposals have been advanced for the creation of a new agency with overall responsibility for internally displaced populations, the designation of an existing agency, or strengthening the existing system of coordination.

## A New Agency

The reasoning runs as follows: in UNHCR, refugees have an agency specifically dedicated to addressing their problems. Aren't internally displaced people refugees too, refugees who haven't crossed a border? So why shouldn't there be an agency for them too?

As it turns out, there are two serious obstacles to the creation of a new agency to deal with internal displacement. One is financial. To be effective, a new agency would have to duplicate many of the functions already being performed for the internally displaced on an ad hoc basis by existing agencies. The expense associated with doing this would be beyond the means of the United Nations at a time when it struggles to cope with deficits and is under pressure to cut back on staff and expenses.

The more serious constraint, however, is sovereignty, which once again emerges as an issue. Primary responsibility for the internally displaced lies with governments because the displaced remain within their own countries. In reality, however, many states that have substantial problems of internal displacement are either unable or unwilling to offer more than token assistance and protection, and some deliberately abuse the displaced and promote forced displacement. This being the case, an agency for the internally displaced would of necessity intrude upon the domestic jurisdiction of states if it were to be effective. Even governments that do not object to international assistance to the internally displaced could view such an agency as a potential threat to their sovereign authority. Conversely, the creation of an agency for the internally displaced could encourage some governments to dump their problems of internal displacement on the agency rather than first trying to deal with the problems themselves.

### Designation of an Existing Agency

If a new agency is not feasible, why not designate one that already has experience in dealing with internally displaced persons? Both legally and operationally, the UN's refugee agency would appear to be the best qualified. The similarities of working with refugees and internally displaced persons are evident. UNHCR has a solid background of experience both in assistance and in protection, and over the years it has developed special expertise in dealing with internally displaced populations.

In 1993 the government of the Netherlands proposed assigning internal displacement to UNHCR, and the representative of the secretary-general for internally displaced persons made a like suggestion. The agency, however, was reluctant. The "magnitude of the problem," High Commissioner Ogata objected, "far exceeds the capacity and resources of any single agency."[2] UNHCR has taken the position that although it is ready to expand its role in regard to the internally displaced, it is opposed to being assigned exclusive responsibility for them.

An alternative candidate, based on the fact that most internally displaced persons are women and children, might be UNICEF. In some respects the agency would appear well suited for the task. It is highly decentralized, which would allow for rapidity of action, and it operates on both sides of conflict zones. Moreover, the agency's international renown would make it difficult for governments or insurgent groups to refuse to cooperate with it.

UNICEF, however, has been primarily a development agency, building water systems, improving medical facilities, and providing innoculations to children. It does not have broad expertise in protection and assistance to uprooted populations in situations of conflict or internal strife. And although it recently has taken steps

---

2. Sadako Ogata, "Statement of the High Commissioner for Refugees to the World Conference on Human Rights," Vienna, June 15, 1993.

to expand protection and assistance to internally displaced women and children, it has made clear that it is not prepared to assume the entire responsibility.

## The Collaborative Approach

The remaining option is coordination of effort by all UN and other humanitarian agencies. Essentially it is the system that has operated since 1992 and that, as we have seen, has given less than satisfactory results. The question is how can it be made more effective?

Making a coordinated system more effective is the goal of the reform program announced by Secretary-General Annan in July 1997. The program retained the emergency relief coordinator as the key element in the system. The ERC continues to chair the Inter-Agency Standing Committee but now also heads a newly created, smaller, and more senior body, the Executive Committee on Humanitarian Affairs (ECHA). The Department of Humanitarian Affairs was terminated and core functions have been integrated into a new Office for the Coordination of Humanitarian Affairs (OCHA), while other elements have been transferred to other agencies. Along with its other mandates, the office of the ERC is given responsibility for ensuring, as part of its coordination functions, that "protection and assistance" for internally displaced persons are addressed. DHA's Geneva-based Task Force on Internally Displaced Persons was disbanded and the more senior Inter-Agency Standing Committee Working Group was designated as the forum for working-level consultations on matters concerning internally displaced populations.

Under the 1997 reforms, as before, responsibility for making the system work rests primarily with the emergency relief coordinator. Although the reforms have strengthened this position, the central weaknesses of earlier years, the ERC's lack of authority to compel action by operational agencies and shortage of funding, persist. Whether the reform program succeeds is likely to depend in large measure on the energy, skill, and dedication of the person appointed to the position.

Late in 1997 Secretary-General Annan designated a new ERC, Sergio Vieira de Mello. One of his first actions was to appoint to OCHA's staff a senior officer to work exclusively on internal displacement and to strengthen liaison with the representative of the secretary-general and officials in other UN agencies who serve as focal points for issues of internal displacement. The initiative is an important one. It appears to augur well for prospects for integrating the internally displaced into emergency programs coordinated by the ERC.

In *Masses in Flight* Cohen and Deng suggest a number of steps for making the collaborative approach more effective in dealing with situations of internal displacement.

—*First,* assign principal responsibility for the internally displaced to *one* operational agency in each emergency. This does not mean that a single agency should by itself attempt to extend the full gamut of assistance and protection to a given internally displaced population; it would mean that one agency would be designated to assume responsibility for monitoring the overall needs of the displaced, for directly addressing some of those needs, and for mobilizing the support of other agencies, backed by an effective interagency coordinating mechanism. Case studies in *The Forsaken People* show that when one agency was designated, as in Tajikistan or in the former Yugoslavia, situations of internal displacement were dealt with more effectively. When no single agency was designated, as in Liberia, Burundi, and Rwanda, internally displaced persons failed to receive adequate attention. Coordination mechanisms alone were found to be ineffective in ensuring adequate protection and assistance to internally displaced populations. Cohen and Deng point out that the organization chosen need not always be a UN agency. In 1995 and 1996 the

International Organization for Migration served as principal agency for providing assistance to internally displaced persons in Somalia, and the International Committee of the Red Cross became the de facto lead agency for the displaced in Chechnya.

—*Second*, encourage agencies to carve out specific areas of expertise in dealing with problems of internal displacement so as to establish a division of labor. For example, when internally displaced persons are congregated in camps and settlements, UNHCR, UNICEF, and WFP would automatically be expected to participate in aiding them. When there are large numbers of children among the internally displaced, UNICEF would be expected to come in.

—*Third*, establish in the Inter-Agency Standing Committee a locus of responsibility and information on internal displacement. The IASC Working Group should monitor all situations of internal displacement, advise on the extent to which the needs of displaced persons are being met, and identify situations where there are serious gaps in the international response. It should develop policy on critical issues, in particular on the coupling of protection with assistance and how resident/humanitarian coordinators can strengthen protection. The Working Group should consider ways to ensure that recommendations made by the representative of the secretary-general on internally displaced persons are carried out. The IASC and its Working Group also need to develop strategies to cope with situations where governments obstruct or refuse access to the international community.

—*Fourth*, integrate protection and assistance more effectively. As UN Secretary-General Annan has observed, "Where security is present, humanitarian aid reaches those who need it . . . where security is absent, humanitarian aid is blocked."[3] Protection

---

3. Kofi Annan, "The Peacekeeping Prescription," in *Preventive Diplomacy*, edited by Kevin M. Cahill (Basic Books, 1996), pp. 178–79.

After the genocide of the summer of 1994, Rwandan Hutus streamed into this camp at Kibeho in search of safety, swelling its population to an estimated 150,000 by early 1995. This picture was taken in the camp in March 1995, one month before the massacre perpetrated by government forces.

Photograph by Sebastiao Salgado.

should be made a core consideration in every humanitarian emergency. Human rights and protection needs should be addressed on an equal level with those relating to providing food, health care, water, and sanitation. In each instance, responsibility for protection should be clearly established. To avoid repetition of the disaster that occurred at Kibeho in Rwanda in 1995—where several thousand were massacred in full view of a UN peacekeeping force—leadership on protection should be clearly defined and a united front presented by the United Nations to governments and insurgent groups. The UN human rights system should be integrated more closely into the protection function and where feasible should assume an operational role through the despatch of human rights field staff.

—*Fifth*, strengthen the position of the representative of the secretary-general on internally displaced persons. Since his appointment the representative has visited thirteen countries with serious problems of internal displacement; undertaken dialogues with governments, international agencies, and nongovernmental organizations; worked to raise awareness of the plight of the internally displaced; stimulated improvements in the international response system; and promoted the development of a legal framework for assistance and protection for the internally displaced.

The representative's position, however, is voluntary and part time, and the resources placed at his disposal by the UN system are minimal. On his own initiative the representative has successfully managed to mobilize financial support for his mandate from outside the United Nations. Still, he lacks the means to undertake systematic monitoring of situations of internal displacement or to ensure that the internally displaced are fully integrated into UN field programs. If the representative is to carry out his mandate effectively, he will need from the United Nations additional human and material resources and strengthened political support in his dealings with governments that seek to avoid scrutiny of serious problems of internal displacement. He will also need clarification and strengthening of his authority to establish direct contacts with insurgent forces that control areas in which large numbers of internally displaced are found.

—*Sixth*, integrate relief and development more effectively. Relief programs should be designed to build capabilities, and development planning should begin early on in an emergency. As Michael Priestly said in a 1994 report to the Department of Humanitarian Affairs, the "traditional dichotomy between relief and development funding and operations" should be abandoned.[4] Humanitarian relief and development agencies should develop plans for rehabilitation together. Cohen and Deng suggest that

---

4. Michael Priestly, "Report to the Under-Secretary-General, Department of Humanitarian Affairs," September 21, 1994, p. 5.

**Francis Deng, representative of the secretary-general, inspects railway cars used to house internally displaced persons in Barda, Azerbaijan, May 1998. At right is Ms. Erin Mooney, Office of the High Commissioner for Human Rights, Geneva.**

Photograph by the UN Department of Public Information (Azerbaijan).

development agencies create a "rehabilitation fund" to be used in postconflict emergency situations where recovery programs do not fit into conventional development or relief categories. Such a fund could help rehabilitate whole populations, whether composed of internally displaced persons, local residents, returnees, or refugees.

## Chapter Six

## Nongovernmental and Regional Organizations

**NGOs and other civil society actors are perceived not only as disseminators of information or providers of services but also as shapers of policy, be it in peace and security matters, in development or in humanitarian affairs.**

Kofi Annan, "Renewing the United Nations: A Programme for UN Reform," July 14, 1997

Agencies of the United Nations may bear the main burden of assisting and protecting the world's internally displaced but two other kinds of organizations have recently emerged to take an important part in humanitarian relief, development, and human rights advocacy: nongovernmental organizations (NGOs) and, in Africa, Europe, and Latin America, regional organizations.

### Nongovernmental Organizations

NGOs have enjoyed enormous success since the end of the cold war, largely owing to their flexibility and speed in responding to emergencies and their deep sense of dedication. They have come to be particularly important in crises of internal displacement. At times, as in Somalia in the initial phase of the crisis, they have been the only ones on the ground. As a result, aid channelled through NGOs by government and public donations has increased to the point where some surpass UN agencies in total dollar value of relief operations. The annual budgets of some of the major international NGOs now reach close to $500 million.

**The knowledge and access that [regional organizations] have in their regions make them likely candidates to become the first line of defense, the first to alert the international community to problems, and the first to seek to avert and resolve crises.**

Roberta Cohen and
Francis M. Deng, in
*Masses in Flight:
The Global Crisis of
Internal Displacement*

NGOs likewise have become the main implementing partners of UN agencies in emergency situations. They are to be found delivering humanitarian assistance, setting up water and sanitation systems, and providing reintegration and development support in virtually every significant humanitarian crisis worldwide.

But their very numbers pose problems. There are estimated to be about forty international NGOs—twenty in the United States and twenty in Europe—sufficiently involved in what the UN calls "complex emergencies" to have a substantial impact. But in any given situation dozens more may show up to offer their services, overwhelming host governments and creating serious problems of coordination. For unlike UN agencies, NGOs are completely separate entities, without organizational ties, joint funding appeals, or common standards. The services of some may target a particular religious or ethnic group to the exclusion of others in need. In the absence of effective coordination they may work at cross-purposes or leave serious needs unattended. The assistance they offer has in some cases been thought inadvertently to prolong conflicts by permitting belligerents to continue fighting while the NGOs care for the civilian population.

For coordination, nongovernmental organizations generally look to the United Nations and to the host government. They have not always been satisfied with what they find. Most NGOs surveyed for *Masses in Flight* believed that the United Nations should designate an operational focal point with a clear mandate for coordination in situations of internal displacement; or that an existing UN agency, such as the UNHCR, should be given the authority and resources to direct UN and NGO efforts. The organizations also have begun to try to coordinate their own activities. In Mozambique and Afghanistan, an NGO umbrella organization was set up to act as focal point with the United Nations. In Rwanda, Save the Children Fund US became the focal point.

Nongovernmental organizations have also begun to develop common standards and rules of behavior to guide their operations. A code of conduct drawn up in 1994 for the International Red Cross and Red Crescent Movement and NGOs in disaster relief has won the adherence of 104 organizations.

## An NGO Dilemma: To Assist Only, or to Assist and Protect?

Traditionally NGOs that have engaged in providing relief and development assistance to disaster stricken populations have considered protection and the monitoring of human rights abuses to be outside their mandate. The common view has been that keeping people alive by providing food and medical supplies ensures their most basic human right, and that by their presence alone NGOs discourage governments or rebel organizations from perpetrating serious human rights abuses. Most have been reluctant to engage in activities such as collecting and forwarding information on human rights violations, intervening with governments, and publicly condemning violations. The most common explanation offered is fear that intervention on human rights grounds would put their staff members at personal risk and their organizations at risk of expulsion.

Such need not always be the case. Two major organizations have policies that go beyond the traditional stance and in effect constitute providing protection. Médecins Sans Frontières, the Francophone European medical group, has a policy of "temoignage," or witnessing, which includes establishing presence near people in danger, reporting on their condition, and publicly condemning massive and repeated violations of human rights and humanitarian law. The World Council of Churches has a policy on uprooted people that calls for a wide range of protection activ-

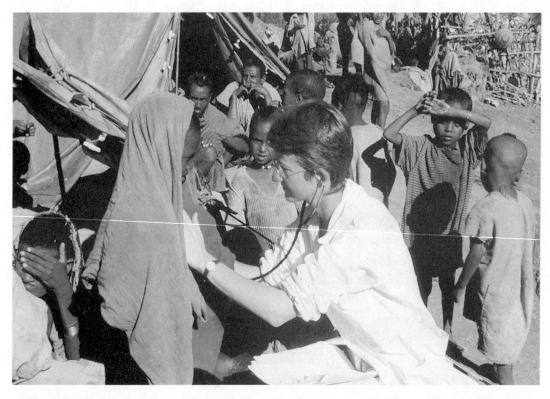

**A Médecins Sans Frontières doctor examines an internally displaced child in Sudan, October 1991.**

Photograph by Médecins Sans Frontières.

ities, including advocacy, the provision of sanctuary and legal aid, conflict resolution, and the monitoring of returns. Overall, their protection policies have enhanced rather than detracted from their effectiveness.

Other NGOs, while hesitant to move so far, have come to realize that a policy of silence risks making them accomplices to serious human rights abuses. Most of those surveyed for *Masses in Flight* were interested in knowing how they could work more effectively to improve protection for internally displaced populations. The organizations themselves offered the following suggestions.

—Design assistance programs to promote protection. Attention to camp layout; the placement of lighting, latrines, and water pumps; and the erection of simple security barriers can go a long way toward strengthening security.

—Engage internally displaced persons in protection programs. Provide information to them and to the surrounding community and local officials. In particular, programs should be developed to protect women against sexual violence, provide legal counseling, and help with documentation.

—Increase field staff presence when protection problems arise. This should be done immediately rather than waiting until a situation is out of hand. Human rights NGOs should be encouraged to second field staff to humanitarian organizations working with internally displaced populations deemed to be at particular risk.

—Communicate information on protection problems to those who can act on it. If unable themselves to act on human rights abuses that they witness, NGOs should pass their information on to others, in particular those that specialize in human rights and protection, who can then use it without revealing the sources.

—Coordinate protection activities better. In-country task forces composed of UN agencies and NGOs could be created that focus not only on assistance but also on protection. NGOs can protect themselves from government retaliation by adopting joint positions on protection issues. One vocal organization can easily be singled out for expulsion, but it is much harder for a government to take punitive measures against all nongovernmental organizations.

—Support community-based protection. Activities that encourage the restoration of communal links or promote the integration of internally displaced persons into the surrounding community can contribute to their security.

—Ensure that NGO programs are consistent with the human rights of the beneficiaries and surrounding communities. Regularly review and assess programs to determine the extent to which assistance is reaching the intended beneficiaries, whether the assistance is lending legitimacy to a repressive regime or insurgent group, and whether the operation reinforces discriminatory or harmful practices, particularly against women.

—Establish training programs for operational staff, both for humanitarian and human rights organizations. Humanitarian NGOs should be given training in human rights standards and humanitarian law and in the Guiding Principles on Internal Displacement discussed in the next chapter. Human rights organization staffs would benefit from training in humanitarian standards and operations. Training courses could be offered by the Office of the UN High Commissioner for Human Rights and by UNHCR and ICRC.

Above and beyond the contribution that international NGOs can make in carrying out assistance and protection programs for the internally displaced, they have a potentially important one to make in fostering ties with and building capacities of local counterparts. Local organizations have roots in the local culture, interact closely with local authorities, and have much needed information about internally displaced populations. Often they are the only ones in place to carry on after the departure of international agencies.

Building local NGO capacities, however, is not always easy. In some countries, local organizations are capable and active, but in others—in the former Soviet Union, for instance, where there was no tradition of organization outside the framework of government—they are administratively weak, technically inexperienced, and lacking in financial management capability. Donors and international organizations have increasingly sought to encourage international NGOs to involve local partners in their work. The development of a worldwide information system on internal displacement, a project being undertaken by the Norwegian Refugee Council, should help identify local groups and strengthen ties between international and local NGOs.

**Muslim women and children in a displaced persons camp in eastern Croatia in 1994 waiting for mail distribution from relatives and friends who remained behind in the Bihac pocket.**

Photograph by Sebastiao Salgado.

Above all, UN agencies should not simply use nongovernmental organizations to carry out their programs but should recognize them as partners and engage them fully in the development of policies and in operational decisions affecting the internally displaced. Failure to do so can have serious consequences, as in Kenya in 1995 when UN agencies are said by Human Rights Watch-Africa to have worked exclusively with the government and to have ignored local NGOs, with disastrous results.

Finally, vigilance is needed to ensure that the growing reliance of international NGOs on governments and international organizations for funding not affect their independence, weaken their role as critics, or affect where they go and the extent of their involvement.

## Regional Organizations

Internal conflict and large-scale human rights violations almost always have an impact at the regional level. Displacement attendant on civil war often finds its outlet in refugee flows. Neighboring states suffer economic and political dislocations, and at times conflict itself spreads across borders. Governments generally look to international organizations for support. Such support, while often provided, is far from assured. In the crises in Liberia, Rwanda, and Somalia little or no UN or other international action was forthcoming during critical periods.

In a model international humanitarian response system, regional organizations would assume significant responsibility for their areas. They would become the first line of defense, alerting the international community to problems and seeking to avert or resolve crises. They would lend active assistance to international organizations in dealing with internal displacement, in particular with protection and prevention.

Needless to say, this model is far from reality. Nonetheless, regional organizations have begun to become involved in conflict prevention and problems of mass displacement, although their efforts are for the most part still rudimentary. Here is where matters stand in each geographic region.

### Africa

Africa's regional body, the Organization of African Unity, founded in 1963 and headquartered in Addis Ababa, Ethiopia, was long mainly a political organization that dealt with disputes between states and championed pan-African causes. Problems within states were considered off limits. But in recent years, as the continent's internally displaced populations have grown to 10 million, the taboo against looking at how a state treats its own population has weakened and the OAU has begun to address the issue of internal displacement.

In 1993 the OAU set up a Mechanism for Conflict Prevention, Management and Resolution together with a conflict prevention center. The conflict prevention efforts met with success in the Congo (Brazzaville) in 1993, when the organization brokered an agreement between rival political groups, and in the OAU's sponsorship of the 1993 accords on Rwanda. When the military overthrew the elected government of Burundi, the OAU initiated sanctions and sent an observer mission.

In 1994 the organization declared internal displacement to be "one of the most tragic humanitarian and human rights crises in Africa today." OAU Secretary-General Salim Ahmed Salim called on the organization to work with international humanitarian and human rights organizations to promote protection and assistance for internally displaced persons and advocated greater OAU involvement in preventing conflicts.

In general, however, the OAU has moved cautiously, mostly owing to its emphasis on sovereignty and noninterference in internal affairs. OAU members have shied away from proposals to create an African peacekeeping force. The organization has done nothing to address the massive problem of internal displacement in Sudan and has played no significant role in the crises in Liberia, Sierra Leone, the Democratic Republic of the Congo, and Angola. So far it has limited itself mainly to sponsoring meetings to raise awareness of the continent's problems of internal displacement. The OAU's main bodies dealing with refugees, the Commission on Refugees, Returnees and Displaced Persons and the Bureau for Refugees, Displaced Persons and Humanitarian Affairs, essentially have not gone beyond holding meetings to call attention to Africa's problems of internal displacement.

The commission might take the following steps to be more effective.

—Ask governments to provide information on their laws and practices with regard to the internally displaced.

—Undertake missions to countries with serious problems of internal displacement and issue reports and recommendations.

—Appoint a special rapporteur on internal displacement.

—Under Article 58 of the African Charter, alert the OAU Assembly to situations of internal displacement.

OAU action is hindered also by a serious shortage of resources. The organization's annual budget is only $30 million and the budget of the Bureau for Refugees and Displaced Persons is limited to 2 percent of that figure. A way around that limitation might be for the bureau to be authorized to solicit funds directly from governments and foundations.

Three subregional organizations have begun to help avert and resolve conflicts in Africa and to some extent promote assistance, protection, and development for the internally displaced. Foremost among these is the Economic Community of West African States, ECOWAS. Through its military intervention in the Liberian civil war from 1990 onward, the organization became directly involved in protecting internally displaced populations. Its record is not unblemished; soldiers of ECOMOG, the ECOWAS military mission, are reported to have engaged at times in rampant looting and assaults on the population it was supposed to protect. ECOMOG won praise, however, for establishing a modicum of security first in Monrovia and later more broadly. It took no hand in providing assistance to the displaced, but it did provide protection, and its presence in Monrovia made possible the return of UN and other humanitarian personnel in the fall of 1990 after their hasty evacuation earlier in the year.

The specific lesson to be drawn from ECOWAS's action in Liberia is that such intervention should be subject to oversight by and coordination with the OAU and the UN and that intervening

**Fighting in the interior of Liberia in 1990 caused large numbers of persons to seek safety in Monrovia. The crowd here awaits food distribution at a center for internally displaced persons.**

Photograph by Hiram Ruiz, U.S. Committee for Refugees.

military forces should have training in observing human rights and humanitarian law.

The subregional body for Southern Africa, the Southern African Development Community has been involved in conflict prevention and resolution and, indirectly at least, has helped ease problems of internal displacement. SADC has contributed to the resolution of conflicts in Mozambique, Zimbabwe, and Angola, as a result of which hundreds of thousands of refugees and internally displaced persons have been able to return home.

An East African subregional body, the Inter-Governmental Authority on Development has become involved in conflict resolution in the Horn of Africa, primarily in Somalia and Sudan. IGAD's basic role has been to help member states overcome the effects of drought and other natural disasters, but it has recently expressed willingness to collaborate with UN development programs in reintegrating uprooted populations.

## Europe

It was only with the end of the cold war that Europe, a continent with an estimated 5 million internally displaced, got an effective regional body. The Organization for Security and Cooperation in Europe (OSCE), formerly the Conference on Security and Cooperation in Europe, includes all the countries of eastern and western Europe as well as Turkey, along with the United States and Canada, fifty-five members in all. It has evolved into an operational institution that seeks to prevent, manage, and resolve conflicts within states.

Among the OSCE's preventive diplomacy tools is the regular dispatch of missions to troubled areas to mediate disputes. It also deploys missions of "long duration" to ease local tensions, encourage dialogue and reconciliation, and promote the development of democratic institutions. Long-term OSCE missions have been stationed in Macedonia, Moldova, Estonia, Latvia, Georgia, and other areas. In 1992 the organization appointed a High Commissioner for National Minorities, an important step, since in Europe the great bulk of the internally displaced are minorities.

Although the OSCE considers conflict prevention and resolution a prime means of averting mass displacement, it has yet to develop a specific policy or program for the internally displaced. It has nonetheless had to confront the problem through its missions to Tajikistan—where in 1995 the organization took over monitoring from UNHCR of the safety and human rights of internally displaced persons returning to their home areas—Bosnia and Herzegovina, Nagorno-Karabakh, and Chechnya. The OSCE has however given scant attention to Turkey, the country with the largest internally displaced population in the region but

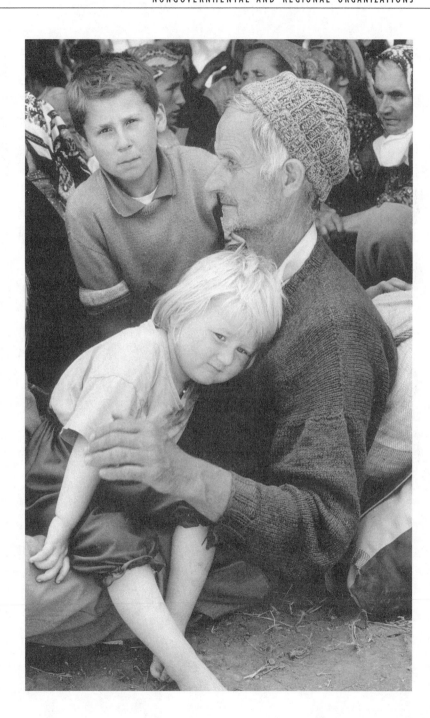

These Bosnian Muslims fled their homes in Zepa as the town came under Serbian attack in 1995 and walked ten kilometers through combat zones to reach safety in Zenica, central Bosnia.

Photograph by Sebastiao Salgado.

**An old trailer near Yevlakh, Azerbaijan, was the only shelter that this Azeri family, displaced by fighting in 1994 between Armenia and Azerbaijan, could find.**

Photograph by A. Hollmann, Office of the UN High Commissioner for Refugees.

whose government has resisted both international and regional involvement.

The OSCE could strengthen its effectiveness in matters relating to internal displacement by

—defining internal displacement as a "human dimension" issue with which the organization should become involved, articulating a policy toward situations of internal displacement, and reviewing government compliance;

—developing an information base on internal displacement within the region and having missions routinely collect information on forced displacement;

—having long-term missions seek to promote the development of national institutions, laws, and policies to help protect, assist, and reintegrate the internally displaced;

—developing a cadre of monitors trained in protection and human rights to deploy to areas of displacement; and

—taking a stronger position on the obligation of OSCE member states to honor their human rights protection and other commitments. This should include initiatives with governments whose policies lead to mass displacement, notably Turkey and, in the matter of Chechnya, Russia.

The OSCE could also seek the assistance of other European regional or subregional organizations, notably the European Union and the Council of Europe, in promoting assistance and protection for internally displaced populations.

## The Americas

With the end of the cold war and the resolution of civil wars in Central America, the number of internally displaced people in the Americas has declined dramatically. Nonetheless, the region still counts 2 million to 3 million internally displaced. Serious problems of internal displacement continue in Guatemala, Peru, and in particular Colombia.

The Organization of American States, the hemisphere's regionwide organization, has focused principally on the defense of democracy. Although its efforts have helped reduce the potential for massive displacement, the organization has done little to deal specifically with internal displacement beyond acknowledging the existence of the problem.

The spearhead for action on internal displacement within the OAS has been the Inter-American Commission on Human Rights. The commission is composed of seven independent legal experts. It has developed into an effective body for investigating and disclosing human rights abuses in OAS member states. In a report on Guatemala in 1994 it called on the government to cease military harassment of the displaced and to extend them legal recognition. In a report on the forcible displacement of Miskito

**Huts built on steep hillsides by internally displaced families near Medellin, Colombia, could easily be washed away by a heavy rainstorm.**

Photograph by Hiram Ruiz, U.S. Committee for Refugees.

Indians in Nicaragua, the commission recommended that compensation be awarded them for the damage to their property. In 1996, upon the recommendation of the representative of the UN secretary-general on internally displaced persons, the commission appointed a special rapporteur on internally displaced persons.

Other steps the OAS commission might consider are to

—press the OAS General Assembly to set up mechanisms to monitor national programs and remedies for the internally displaced and organize technical assistance where needed;

—adopt an emergency procedure so that when severe internal displacement develops, an emergency mission could be sent, an urgent action report issued, and staff deployed to the field to help prevent violations and increase protection;

—make known to displaced populations how to bring cases before the commission and bring problems of internal displacement before the Inter-American Court of Human Rights; and

—develop joint strategies with international bodies and with the representative of the secretary-general.

Outside the OAS framework, internal displacement has been the focus of a unique initiative: the Permanent Consultation on Internal Displacement in the Americas, or CPDIA in its Spanish initials. The organization was established in 1992 by the Inter-American Institute of Human Rights and is made up of representatives from international organizations such as UNHCR, UNDP, UNICEF, WFP, and IOM and nongovernmental organizations and research institutes. It is designed to collect information on internally displaced persons, analyze specific country situations and make recommendations for solutions, provide technical assistance to governments and organizations working with the displaced, and promote respect for the human rights of displaced populations through meetings, forums, and educational and training programs. It has produced a draft body of legal principles applicable to the internally displaced, undertaken two missions to Colombia and one to Guatemala, and developed recommendations for improving the situation of the internally displaced in those countries. It has also lent support to grassroots projects for the displaced.

CPDIA is unique in bringing together human rights and humanitarian bodies and intergovernmental and nongovernmental organizations and drawing on their combined expertise in dealing with problems of internal displacement. It merits emulation in other regions.

## The Middle East and Asia

Unlike Africa, Europe, and the Americas, neither the Middle East nor Asia counts an all-encompassing regional organization. The

League of Arab States, based in Cairo and comprising twenty-two members, excludes Iran and Israel and spills over into Saharan and sub-Saharan Africa. The only working regional groups within Asia are subregional organizations: the Association of Southeast Asian Nations (ASEAN) and the South Asian Association for Regional Cooperation (SAARC).

Since the late 1940s the Arab League has focused its attention almost exclusively on the needs of externally and internally displaced Palestinians. It has ignored serious problems of internal displacement affecting non-Arab minority groups within its region, particularly in Sudan and Iraq. Voices have nonetheless been raised in the Arab world to urge the Arab League to undertake broader activities on behalf of internally displaced persons and refugees. In 1992 a group of Arab experts issued a call for Arab governments to provide the organization's secretariat with information and statistics on the condition of refugees and displaced persons in their countries and the national laws, regulations, and decrees in force relating to them. In 1995 a conference held in Tripoli, Lebanon, recommended that each Arab state create institutions to deal with internal displacement.

For more than ten years the United Nations has tried to encourage the development of regional human rights machinery in Asia. Divergent political, economic, and social systems, and ideological differences and the opposition of China, the region's largest and most powerful state, have blocked the proposal.

ASEAN's declared purpose is to promote regional stability and economic and social cooperation. It has discussed refugee issues, in particular mass exoduses from Indochina, but its main interest has been in curtailing refugee flows and repatriating nonrefugees. Internal displacement has not figured on its agenda and is unlikely to do so in the near future. In fact several ASEAN governments have argued in international conferences that action on issues in the domestic sphere of states constitutes an unacceptable infringement on state sovereignty. SAARC also has not involved itself in problems of internal displacement, despite the large numbers of displaced in Sri Lanka and displacement caused by the conflict in Kashmir.

For the most part, regional institutions have not yet developed adequate capacities to become significant factors in situations of internal displacement. Nonetheless, the past half decade has witnessed a growing awareness in some regions of the need to address the problem. The next step will be to strengthen these initiatives and develop a system of shared responsibility with international organizations. One way to promote cooperation between regional and international bodies might be for the UN secretary-general, the representative of the secretary-general on internally displaced persons, and the UN's senior humanitarian and human rights officials to meet with the heads of regional organizations to discuss measures to be taken in emergencies. For Asia, where no continentwide regional organization exists, the UN Economic and Social Commission for Asia and the Pacific could be assigned a role in dealing with problems of internal displacement. UN workshops on the promotion of human rights in Asia could also explore ways of advancing regional protection for the internally displaced.

# A Legal Framework for Protecting the Internally Displaced

**I owned plot number 938 in Chegamba village . . . I was chased off my land during the ethnic clashes and the original title deed was burnt. In February 1996 . . . I went to the Commission of Land, and there I found that the title deed had been transferred. . . . They told me to take [my case] to the courts. How can I? I have no money to even get an affidavit.**

Displaced Kikuyu man, Kenya, in *Failing the Internally Displaced*, Human Rights Watch-Africa, 1997

For those dealing with matters relating to internally displaced persons, it was clear long ago that there was an important legal gap in their protection. Refugees were protected by a detailed international legal code, set out in the 1951 Refugee Convention. This document established effective norms for their treatment, and a 1967 protocol extended their application to areas beyond Europe. But there was no one instrument setting forth the rights of the internally displaced.

Obviously, the internally displaced did not forfeit their rights by the act of becoming displaced. But no one knew just what rights they could legitimately claim and what obligations governments and insurgent forces had toward them. Or beyond that, just where international legal protections for the internally displaced might fall short of providing adequate protection.

No legal document could prevent governments determined to displace or otherwise abuse their citizens from doing so. But the existence of an acknowledged set of standards could have an important deterrent effect. So long as no one knew just what international legal rights applied to the internally displaced, it was easy to abuse them. If clear, recognized legal norms could be assembled, governments, international organizations, and non-governmental organizations would know what standards are applicable; and governments and insurgent forces might be more hesitant to risk being found in violation of the standards.

With these considerations in mind, and with the support of foundations and governments, in 1994 the representative of the secretary-general enlisted the expertise of the American Society of International Law, the International Human Rights Law Group, the American College of Law of the American University, and the Ludwig Boltzmann Institute of Human Rights in Vienna, Austria. The task was to compile the relevant provisions of international human rights law, humanitarian law, and refugee law and analyze how they apply to the protection and assistance of internally displaced persons. A working group was assembled under the leadership of Robert Kogod Goldman, professor of law at the Washington College of Law and codirector of its Center for Human Rights and Humanitarian law; Walter K. Kalin, professor of constitutional and international law at the University of Bern, Switzerland, and former dean of its School of Law; and Manfred Nowak, director of the Ludwig Boltzmann Institute. Legal experts from the International Committee of the Red Cross, UN High Commissioner for Refugees, and UN Centre for Human Rights joined in. In meetings over the next year and one-half in Geneva, Vienna, and Washington, the working group developed a comprehensive Compilation and Analysis of Legal Norms.

The document found that although there is extensive coverage for the displaced under international law there are also significant areas in which the law fails to provide sufficient coverage. The working group identified four categories of gaps.

—Normative gaps, where international law fails to provide any protection for particular needs. For example, the law is silent on restitution of property lost as a consequence of displacement during armed conflict or to compensation for its loss.

—Applicability gaps, in which a legal norm exists but is not applicable in all circumstances. For example, in some situations of tension and disturbances, humanitarian law does not apply and human rights law may be ignored.

—Consensus gaps, in which a general norm exists but a more specific right has not yet been articulated to ensure implementation in areas of particular need to the internally displaced. For instance, a general norm prohibits cruel and inhuman treatment but does not specify that internally displaced persons must not be forceably returned to conditions of danger.

—Ratification gaps, where states have signed but not ratified (or neither signed nor ratified) key human rights treaties or the Geneva Conventions and are therefore not bound by their provisions, except to the extent that the treaties have attained the status of customary law.

In addition to gaps in the law, the Compilation and Analysis of Legal Norms identified seventeen areas of insufficient protection. To remedy these, it suggested that any future restatement of the law should include a specific protection against the forced return of internally displaced persons to places of danger. It called for specific protections for internally displaced women and children. It urged restrictions on the lawful detention of internally displaced persons in closed camps. It recommended the creation of a right to restitution or compensation for property lost as a consequence of displacement in situations of armed conflict, and recognition of the need of the displaced for personal identification, documentation, and registration. And it pointed up the need to recognize an explicit obligation on the part of governments to accept offers of humanitarian assistance and protect relief workers, their transports, and their supplies.

Francis Deng presented the Compilation and Analysis to the Commission on Human Rights at its 1996 session. It was favorably received by commission members as well as by intergovernmental organizations and nongovernmental organizations. The United Nations disseminated the Compilation and Analysis through publication as a sales document. The UNHCR developed a manual for its field staff based on the document.

The next step, building on the Compilation and Analysis of Legal Norms, was to develop a legal framework for the internally displaced. Both the Commission on Human Rights and the UN General Assembly gave Deng backing to proceed in that direction. As the legal team worked during 1996 and 1997 to develop a document, it consulted representatives of the United Nations and other intergovernmental and nongovernmental organizations.

Some initially questioned the need for a body of principles specifically applicable to the internally displaced. It was argued that the development of new standards could detract from efforts to implement the standards that already exist. Concern also was expressed that a normative framework specifically tailored to the needs of the internally displaced could result in discrimination against other groups.

In answer to these objections, it was pointed out that provisions abound in international law for special protections for disadvantaged groups—whether refugees, minorities, indigenous populations, the disabled, or women and children. A body of guiding principles tailored to the needs of the internally displaced would not discriminate against others but would ensure that internally displaced persons are protected and their unique needs addressed. Guiding principles were needed to make existing provisions of law more explicit, fill gaps and illuminate grey areas, and bring together in one place the whole of law applicable to the internally displaced. It was also necessary to raise international awareness of the needs of internally displaced persons and give humanitarian and human rights bodies a document to turn to when advocating on their behalf.

The Guiding Principles on Internal Displacement were finalized at a 1998 meeting in Vienna of international legal experts and representatives of UN agencies, regional bodies, and nongovernmental organizations, hosted by the government of Austria. The text of the Guiding Principles is appended to this volume. They apply both to governments and insurgent forces and deal with all phases of displacement. They offer protection against displacement, protection during displacement, and protection during return and reintegration.

Although the Guiding Principles reflect and are consistent with international law, Deng and his colleagues deliberately chose not to seek for them the status of a binding legal document. It was felt that a nonbinding instrument would be the most realistic and also the quickest way to proceed. The instrument could attain authority through use and help create the moral and political climate needed for improved protection and assistance for the internally displaced while avoiding confrontation with governments opposed to binding rules. The Guiding Principles could lead to the development of a binding legal instrument if such were to be considered necessary.

Already the Guiding Principles have begun to make an impact. International humanitarian agencies and nongovernmental organizations have begun to disseminate them. At its 1998 annual session, the Commission on Human Rights adopted a resolution taking note of the Guiding Principles and acknowledging the stated intention of the representative to use them in his work. Earlier, the

Inter-Agency Standing Committee welcomed the principles and encouraged its member agencies to share them with their executive boards and staff and apply them in their work. Both the Inter-American Commission on Human Rights of the Organization of American States and the Organization of African Unity have acknowledged the principles and expressed their intention to apply them in the field.

# Chapter Eight

# Strategies and Solutions

War and
displacement have
strongly affected
what was once a
decent, educated
society. There is
much mental
anguish resulting
from deaths,
displacement,
destruction of
property, dispersal.
I don't know how
long it will take
to rebuild.

Community leader
in Jaffna, Sri Lanka,
in "Conflict and
Displacement
in Sri Lanka,"
U.S. Committee
for Refugees, 1997

To this point, we have looked at who and where are the internally displaced, at who helps them and how well or how poorly, and what legal protections they should enjoy—the easy part, one might say. It is time now to turn to the difficult essential: what more needs to be done? How can the international community improve its response to serious cases of internal displacement, make it more effective, and prevent large numbers of displaced from being left out? And finally, what are the solutions?

From their study of internal displacement in its various aspects, Roberta Cohen and Francis Deng draw one overarching conclusion: too much attention has focused on the delivery of emergency assistance. To be effective, they write in *Masses in Flight,*

> strategies to address mass displacement need to be broader and more comprehensive. They should also encompass prevention, protection, and political and economic solutions. The provision of humanitarian assistance should go hand in hand with efforts to advocate for and protect the physical safety and the human rights of the affected popu-

lations. It should be accompanied by political initiatives to resolve conflicts and by plans for reintegration and development. . . . The remedies designed should not only be a response to emergency needs but should seek to prevent the conditions that caused the problem.

Let us look at these elements one by one.

## First: Prevention

Can crises of internal displacement be prevented? Certainly not without first knowing where they are likely to happen. There must be a mechanism to sound the alarm, to alert the international community—the United Nations and its humanitarian and human rights agencies, governments, regional organizations, and nongovernmental organizations—to potential situations of conflict as well as provide information on continuing crises of displacement.

The need for an early warning and information gathering system has been on the UN agenda for years without, however, yet having come to satisfactory resolution. A UN interagency committee that met in 1993 and 1994, the Consultation on Early Warning of New Mass Flows of Refugees and Displaced Persons, identified situations and forwarded warnings to the secretary-general and the heads of UN humanitarian agencies. But these consisted only of naming the country concerned without any accompanying plan of action. Subsequently the Department of Humanitarian Affairs developed a database on some one hundred countries as part of its Humanitarian Early Warning System. However, it took few steps to ensure early action.

Information needs to be gathered not just on the numbers of internally displaced but about prospects for prevention, the access of the displaced to existing services, protection concerns, the capacity and willingness of governments to address needs, and the ability of the international community to offer an effective response.

International human rights and humanitarian nongovernmental organizations are critically important in accomplishing this. They must be closely integrated into the early warning and information gathering mechanism. With their extensive field networks, they are in a position to provide critical information on developing or existing situations of internal displacement. There should be links also with regional organizations, which by their very nature are closer to events than UN bodies and which should be encouraged to develop their own early warning capacities.

Advantage should also be taken of the reports of the UN Human Rights Commission's rapporteurs, a frequently neglected resource. A case in point: almost a year before the April–May 1994 genocide in Rwanda, a commission special rapporteur warned of preparations for genocidal massacre and recommended swift and decisive measures to stave off the impending crisis. The report, however, was not placed on the agenda of the early warning consultation or drawn to the attention of other elements of the United Nations.

How to prevent such oversight? In *Masses in Flight* Cohen and Deng suggest that the UN High Commissioner for Human Rights be empowered to bring reports of urgent and massive human rights violations to the attention of the Security Council and make recommendations for international response.

Following his appointment late in 1997, new Emergency Relief Coordinator Sergio Vieira de Mello set out to fill the gap in information and early warning on internal displacement. As ERC, de Mello is the UN's designated reference point for problems of internal displacement. The best method, it was determined, was to combine the abilities of the UN system with those of a nongovernmental organization. De Mello's office contracted with the

Norwegian Refugee Council to create a database for internal displacement to serve the United Nations as well as the international community.

Why put this important task in the hands of a nongovernmental organization? In addition to flexibility, NGOs are less subject to political constraint than the United Nations and its agencies, which are ultimately answerable to governments and often must rely on information provided by governments. NGOs can probe alternative sources and challenge questionable government data. The Norwegian Refugee Council has been in the forefront of those concerned with issues of internal displacement. In 1998 it published the first detailed global survey on internal displacement.

It is to be hoped that the NRC's database will bring together relevant information on internal displacement in all countries with serious problems and that it will include information on the extent to which national, regional, and international efforts are addressing the needs of the internally displaced. If properly structured, its reports should be of immense assistance to the international community in identifying gaps in prevention, assistance, and protection.

### Good Governance

The only sound and lasting basis for prevention of internal displacement is good governance. Crises of displacement inevitably stem from a failure on the part of governments to discharge their responsibilities to their citizens through good and legitimate governance. In practice this means respect for human rights—understood as the entire spectrum of universal norms, ranging from civil and political rights to economic, social, and cultural rights to minority rights. A system of governance that is responsive to the needs of its population for justice and general well-being offers the best way to safeguard against crises of displacement.

Minority protection is particularly important. Conflicts between governments and minorities are one of the main causes of internal displacement, in particular in Africa, Europe, and Asia. In 1992 the United Nations adopted a Declaration on the Rights of Persons Belonging to National or Ethnic, Religious or Linguistic Minorities, which although nonbinding is the first universal instrument for the protection of minorities. At the regional level, Europe has taken several significant steps. In 1992 the Council of Europe adopted the European Charter for Regional or Minority Languages. In 1995 the council went an important step further in adopting its Framework Convention for the Protection of National Minorities, the first multilateral treaty pertaining exclusively to the protection of national minorities. The council and the Organization for Security and Cooperation in Europe have developed systems for monitoring minority protection, and the OSCE's high commissioner for national minorities, appointed in 1992, has been instrumental in preventing the escalation of several disputes. No other region has comparable machinery, although the initiation of a "Helsinki process" for Africa is under discussion.

Of course, the 1948 Genocide Convention commits states to prevent "acts committed with intent to destroy, in whole or in part, a national, ethnical, racial or religious group." The convention, however, lacks an enforcement mechanism, and the political will to prevent or halt violence against ethnic groups has in most cases not been forthcoming. Consequently, the United Nations and regional organizations need to strengthen—or, where they do not exist, adopt—procedures for containing and resolving conflicts involving minorities.

The most important elements of good governance are an independent judiciary, an uncorrupted civil service and parliament, free and fair elections, a police force and a military respectful of human rights, free functioning nongovernmental organizations, and independent media.

The judiciary is of primary importance because the absence of an effective judicial system makes it almost impossible to ensure the implementation of human rights protections and the redress of violations that cause displacement. The UN High Commissioner for Human Rights has developed programs for training judges, law enforcement officers, and other officials in human rights protections. The OSCE has conducted programs for the strengthening of judicial systems in several of its member countries.

Strengthening civil society at the grassroots offers another counterbalance against the kind of social unrest that produces displacement. One way to do this is through bolstering local NGOs. They are usually the first to become aware of conditions that threaten displacement. Regional organizations should also take a hand in strengthening the capacity of local organizations. The OSCE has been in the forefront of efforts to encourage local NGO networks, and its efforts offer a model for other regional bodies. International NGOs, particularly the Open Society Institute, have also helped develop and strengthen local NGOs, especially in the former Soviet Union.

Obviously, it would be a mistake to argue that good governance can be imposed from outside. It would be equally mistaken, however, to consider that little or nothing can or should be done to encourage its growth. The task is one that calls on the combined skills of international and regional agencies and of nongovernmental organizations.

### Strengthened Legal Protections

The legal basis for preventing displacement also needs to be strengthened through the articulation of a legal right not to be arbitrarily displaced. Such provision should make explicit what is already inherent in international law, offer protection, and provide a basis for actions to prevent such displacement.

**Roadside encampments were the impromptu home for thousands of Azeris internally displaced by fighting between Azerbaijan and Armenia in the summer of 1994.**

Photograph by R. Redmond, Office of the UN High Commissioner for Refugees.

A model for the articulation of a right not to be arbitrarily displaced is offered in the Guiding Principles (see the appendix). They explicitly state, for example, that displacement is prohibited when it is based on policies of apartheid, "ethnic cleansing," or other practices "aimed at or resulting in altering the ethnic, religious or racial composition of the affected population." They also consider as arbitrary displacement the uprooting caused by large development projects that are not justified by compelling and overriding public interests. They further specify that displacement should not be carried out in a manner that violates the rights to life, dignity, liberty, or the security of those affected.

All these are essential components for any international legal statute articulating a right not to be internally displaced.

## Conflict Prevention

The adage "an ounce of prevention is worth a pound of cure" appears yet to be fully appreciated in the international arena. The United Nations, whose founding purpose was to prevent war, has acted mainly to address the consequences of conflict rather than its causes. And the UN's mandate is for conflicts between or among states rather than within states, which is where most conflicts and most internal displacement have occurred since the end of the cold war. True, the UN has over the past decade become more willing to intervene in internal conflicts, but it has paid hardly any attention to prevention. The Security Council did order the preventive deployment of a UN peacekeeping force in Macedonia in 1993 with the aim, so far successful, of safeguarding against extension to that country of the conflagration in Yugoslavia. But when the secretary-general called in 1995 for the dispatch of an international force to avert mass killings in Burundi, he received no response.

One problem is that the United Nations cannot count on any military force being readily at its disposal. Proposals for an international rapid reaction force have consistently failed to win support; this despite the fact that the estimated $200 million annual cost pales by comparison with the more than $1 billion spent by the international community on aid to Rwanda following the failure to act to prevent genocide there. Moreover, the UN's human rights machinery lacks sufficient funding to deploy field staff to prevent or at least minimize the severe human rights violations that lead to displacement.

In recent years there have been some encouraging developments at the regional level. The Organization of African Unity has created a Mechanism for Conflict Prevention, Management and Resolution that aims to anticipate and defuse conflicts. The OAU secretary-general has emphasized the importance of the organization's being able to prevent conflicts from escalating into mass displacement. In Europe, the OSCE has articulated a justification, based on human rights, for intervening in the internal affairs of its member states, and it has deployed field staff with the aim of defusing tensions both between and within states. In Paraguay, Guatemala, and Haiti the Organization of American States has focused on sustaining democratic regimes to prevent human rights violations and stave off conflict.

Still, owing either to lack of resources or lack of will, regional organizations have generally not been able to avert genocide, mass displacement, and other severe problems or tackle intractable civil conflicts. They too lack a standing enforcement capability. In 1994 the OSCE authorized the establishment of a peacekeeping force for Nagorno-Karabakh, but the force never came into being. Proposals for an OAU force have never got beyond the discussion stage. An enforcement capability does exist at the African subregional level in West Africa, where the Economic Community of West African States (ECOWAS) has a mandate to intervene militarily in armed conflict within member states. But its intervention in Liberia, while offering an example of a subregional organization's assuming responsibility for the protection of civilians caught in internal conflict, points up the need for regional bodies and the United Nation to monitor such action to ensure compliance with international standards.

## Second: Integrating Protection with Assistance

Rarely do displaced populations need food, medicine, and shelter alone. Feeding and assisting displaced persons "so that they can survive to be caught in the cross-fire of conflict and acts of ethnic cleansing," in the words of a 1993 UNHCR discussion paper, can hardly be considered effective humanitarian action.[1] Bosnia, where the United Nations was able to deliver food and medicine but unable to provide effective protection, offers a telling example. As one observer put it, the international humanitarian effort there could be considered a success only insofar as it "allowed Bosnians to die on a full stomach."[2]

Standards for the protection of the internally displaced derive from humanitarian and human rights law, from analogous standards in refugee law, and from the practices of the UN High Commissioner for Refugees and other organizations in providing protection. UNHCR has in fact come to apply, on an ad hoc basis, its interpretation of personal security for refugees to the internally displaced. In a variety of situations its staff has monitored the treatment of threatened minority groups, intervened with national authorities to request protective action, investigated and prosecuted specific cases, and helped governments provide personal documentation. In armed conflicts the agency has provided safe passage for civilians, relocated and evacuated them from conflict areas, assisted besieged populations, intervened to prevent the involuntary return of the internally displaced to areas of danger, and alerted goverments and the public to human rights abuses. It has also taken part in mediation and reconciliation efforts between returning displaced persons and local residents.

Similarly, the International Committee of the Red Cross, as custodian of the Geneva Conventions and Protocols, undertakes a

---

1. UN High Commissioner for Refugees, "UNHCR's Role in Protecting and Assisting Internally Displaced People," Central Evaluation Section Discussion Paper EVAL/IDP/13/2 (Geneva, November 1993), para. 77.

2. *Masses in Flight* (Brookings, 1998), p. 255, citing Nicole Gnesotto, "Lessons of Yugoslavia," Chaillot Paper 14 (Paris: Western European Union Institute for Security Studies, 1994), p. 48, in Erin Mooney, "Strategies for Prevention and Protection," paper prepared for Brookings Institution, May 1997.

wide range of activities to protect civilians, including the internally displaced, in situations of armed conflict. ICRC staff are to be found evacuating civilians from areas of danger, creating protected areas, providing assistance, and making representations to goverments and insurgent groups in situations of civil as well as interstate war around the globe.

The Guiding Principles on Internal Displacement for the first time brings together the general principles of protection applicable to internally displaced persons. With wide dissemination and active promotion, the principles can be a helpful tool for field staff of international organizations and NGOs charged with assisting endangered populations.

Looking at protection activities more generally, one can categorize them as running on three levels: community, national, and international.

*Community protection mechanisms* for self-help, civil defense, early warning, and dispute mediation have proven their effectiveness in crises in Africa, Europe, and Latin America. In Somalia in the early 1990s, at the height of civil conflict, local people created organizations to provide educational, health care, and employment services and mediate disputes. In Peru, Colombia, and Guatemala, in the former Yugoslavia and the Caucasus, the internally displaced have organized effectively for self-help and protection.

These community efforts offer a base on which those coming from abroad can build. UN agencies, regional organizations, and NGOs would do well to operate from the premise, as Cohen and Deng put it, that "the internally displaced know better than anyone else how to meet their protection and assistance needs." Reinforcing their efforts could be a promising source of protection. It also could help ensure that programs undertaken by international humanitarian organizations do not unintentionally reinforce repressive authorities or perpetuate discriminatory practices.

At the *national level* some governments have set up agencies to assist the internally displaced and, in particular, help them reintegrate into society. Government action, however, may or may not signal a genuine effort to respond to the needs of the displaced. Usually government agencies to assist them operate with seriously inadequate funding. In some instances the goal has been mainly to promote return, as in Peru where the government has provided support mainly to returnees, neglecting those who wished to resettle. Elsewhere, as in Kenya, Croatia, Cyprus, Azerbaijan, and Georgia, governments have been accused of acting mainly to help a favored ethnic group. Sri Lanka and Lebanon, by contrast, offer more encouraging examples of effective government mechanisms for addressing the needs of the displaced. In particular, when supported and monitored by international organizations and nongovernmental organizations, national institutions—governmental and nongovernmental—can make important contributions to the assistance and protection of internally displaced persons.

When national and community-based protection mechanisms prove inadequate, the task devolves upon the *international community*. The problem at the international level, however, is the one noted earlier—the absence of a clear and automatic locus of responsibility for internally displaced persons. Of the various options discussed, the one that offers the most promise is the designation of an operational focal point for the internally displaced in each complex emergency. UNHCR would be a suitable candidate, but UNICEF, the World Food Programme and, outside the UN system, the ICRC or International Organization for Migration could be equally well qualified depending on the circumstances.

When there is no designated focal point, strong oversight by the resident coordinator or humanitarian coordinator in the field and the Inter-Agency Standing Committee at headquarters will be needed to ensure that agencies work effectively together. Even where there is a designated focal point, the resident or humanitarian coordinators and the IASC will need to monitor the situation closely to see to it that other agencies give the designated agency all required support.

Whether one agency is in charge or there is an interagency coordinated response, human rights protection should be addressed equally with the needs for food, shelter, health care, and sanitation. In case after case it has been shown that assistance cannot be provided effectively without attention to issues of human rights and protection.

Most international humanitarian agencies and nongovernmental organizations rely mainly (and many exclusively) on their physical presence among internally displaced and other at-risk populations to deter abuses and ensure security. Presence can strengthen security, especially where there is cooperation from the government or from insurgent forces. In Sri Lanka UNHCR found its mere physical presence to be an effective restraining influence on the combatants. But in many other instances, presence alone has turned international agencies and NGOs into passive witnesses to killing and other serious abuse.

To be effective, presence must be active. It should include accompaniment, protective custody, neighborhood patrols, protection watches, safe houses, intervention with authorities, and evacuations of those whose lives may be threatened. UNHCR and ICRC routinely engage in such measures, but there is also need for an operational role for human rights bodies. Traditionally, UN human rights bodies have limited their activities to monitoring, reporting, and advocacy. The challenge for these agencies is to take on the broader and more arduous task of working with humanitarian agencies to provide on-site protection in camps and settlements and in monitoring returns. No longer should these UN organizations confine themselves to being simple bookkeepers of horrors; they should take an active hand in mitigating violations and preventing horrors.

The United Nations has taken some important first steps in this direction. UN human rights field staff deployed to Rwanda in 1994 were the first to receive a mandate specifically addressing the protection needs of internally displaced persons returning to their homes. Overall, and notwithstanding the massacre that occurred at the camp in Kibeho in 1995, the Rwanda experience shows that human rights field staff with a mandate for more than mere reporting can truly help internally displaced persons to return home. Beyond facilitating returns, human rights field staff could also serve in designated safe areas and camps in cooperation with humanitarian organizations.

The OSCE and to a lesser extent the European Community have also deployed human rights field staff to protect internally displaced populations. And international human rights NGOs have begun to send out field staff not only to report but to advocate for greater protection and carry out judicial training programs. But such efforts for the most part remain small and exceptional.

The experience in Somalia illustrates just how important it is for protection needs to be integrated into assistance and development programs. There the concentration of food distribution programs in urban areas drew people from the countryside into camps in the main cities where disease and armed gangs flourished. The result was that disease replaced malnutrition as the greatest threat, and the civil war was intensified as people were forced to turn to warlords for protection. And in Kenya the UN Development Programme's failure to include a human rights monitoring component in its program for the return and reintegration of internally displaced persons seriously undermined the program's effectiveness and caused the agency considerable embarrassment.

To avoid such pitfalls, the United Nations should make certain that persons with expertise in human rights and protection are included in interagency needs assessment missions. Interagency discussions held under the umbrella of the Inter-Agency Standing Committee should seek to determine an appropriate division of labor among UN human rights, humanitarian, and development organizations. They should be expected to develop joint strategies in the field for promoting the physical safety and basic human rights of the displaced. Closer collaboration with the representative of the secretary-general on internally displaced persons can also improve protection because the representative can raise protection issues in his dialogues with governments and in his reports to the United Nations.

Nongovernmental organizations also need to design their programs to integrate protection with assistance and development. Those that are unable or unwilling to intervene directly with government authorities to protect the physical safety of populations they assist should at a least communicate information on violations to others who can act on it.

Training is needed, both for NGO and UN personnel, in measures to ensure better protection for endangered populations. The Office of the UN High Commissioner for Human Rights, in cooperation with UNHCR and ICRC, might institute training in law and practical protection measures for organization personnel.

Clearly, however, there comes a point beyond which international humanitarian and human rights organizations and nongovernmental organizations, no matter how well prepared or well intentioned, cannot be expected to carry the burden of protection. In situations of real danger, as in Bosnia, Rwanda, Iraq, or Liberia, civilian staff cannot be expected to do a job that only military intervention can accomplish. When military intervention is authorized, it is essential that it be backed both by all needed force and by the political will to accomplish the task. Relief corridors and safe areas must be defended. In the former Yugoslavia the safe areas of Srebrenica and Zepe were overrun by Serb military units while the United Nations Protection Force stood by.

UN security forces did not have a clear enough mandate or the personnel or equipment required to intervene. Training is also needed to protect endangered populations. And humanitarian and human rights organization staff who work on the ground with security forces should be expected to evaluate the quality of the protection provided by them and to alert world opinion when it is inadequate.

### Women and Children: Special Attention Required

The protection needs of women, who with their children constitute the majority of internally displaced persons, require special attention. The collection of gender-specific information should become a routine part of assessments done by humanitarian and development agencies. When large numbers of displaced women are reported to be facing serious protection problems, special UN evaluation missions should be sent to the field. Although the crisis in Liberia lasted for years and many hundreds of thousands of women were displaced, only once did a UN interagency mission look into the special problems facing them.

Humanitarian and development organizations should be expected to apply to internally displaced women the provisions of UNHCR's guidelines on sexual violence and on the protection of refugee women. Camps should be designed with an eye to meeting women's special security needs, with attention given to the placement of latrines, lighting, and how far women should have to go for firewood. Provision should be made for women's active participation in camp administration and decisionmaking. Too often the response to sexual violence against displaced women focuses on assisting victims after the attack has taken place rather than on preventing violence.

The special protection needs of internally displaced children are also often neglected. In recognition of the inadequacies in the

**Roberta Cohen (right) advocating greater access to credit and income-generating activities for internally displaced women at an OAU seminar in Addis Ababa, October 1998. Mary Maboreke, chief of OAU's Women's Unit, is second from the left.**

Photograph by the UN Economic Commission for Africa.

protection of children, in 1997 the UN secretary-general appointed a special representative on children in armed conflict. Together with UNICEF, the special representative can make assessments of the assistance and protection needs of children and develop strategies for addressing them. UNICEF should be expected to take the lead in the field in extending protection and assistance to internally displaced children. Other agencies also have a responsibility to take measures to protect children, particularly with regard to uniting them with their families, preventing sexual violence against them and their forcible recruitment into armed forces, and promoting psychosocial support for the traumatized.

## Dealing with Sovereignty

Sovereignty, as we have seen earlier, can seriously impede the provision of assistance and protection to the internally displaced. States can fend off intervention from abroad simply by standing on the principle of nonintervention in their internal affairs. A more equitable balance is needed between the sovereignty of states and the equally compelling obligation to provide protection and assistance to the internally displaced and other threatened populations. In the course of their work, UN agencies and non-governmental agencies frequently find themselves confronted with the problem of how to deal with government pressures against humanitarian action.

Francis Deng has been in the forefront of those arguing for the recasting of sovereignty as a concept of responsibility. As he and Roberta Cohen write in *Masses in Flight*,

> Governments by virtue of their sovereignty are obliged to provide for the security and well-being of their populations. When they fail to meet their obligations, they are expected to request outside assistance. Should they refuse to accept such assistance, the legitimacy of their sovereignty can be questioned and the international community should be expected to assert its concern and fill the vacuum created by the government's failure to discharge its responsibility.

UN resolutions have legitimized the establishment of relief corridors and cross-border operations to reach people in need. The United Nations has also insisted on access for delivery of relief and in some cases has authorized the use of force to ensure the delivery of supplies. These resolutions point to the emergence of a right to humanitarian assistance and access when states fail to meet the needs of their citizens and large numbers are at risk.

But is this right matched by a duty on the part of states to accept international offers of humanitarian assistance? *Masses in Flight* advocates the express recognition of such a duty. The Guiding Principles on Internal Displacement stipulate that state consent to the provision of humanitarian assistance "shall not be arbitrarily withheld."

**These Bosnian boys, shown at a displaced persons center in Zenica in 1994, lost their parents and had experienced episodes of shelling and gunfire.**

Photograph by
A. Hollmann,
Office of the UN High
Commissioner for
Refugees.

There are precedents for such provision. In Somalia and the former Yugoslavia the Security Council insisted that there be immediate and unimpeded access by humanitarian organizations to internally displaced and other populations. In Iraq, after determining that there was a threat to international peace and security, the Security Council authorized measures to compel the acceptance of international assistance. The council's failure to support the secretary-general's proposal for an international force for Burundi in 1996 was due less to its solicitude for Burundi's sovereignty (its government opposed the force) than to concern that the costs and risks of intervention would be too high.

In other instances, however, deference to the power—or the sheer stubbornness—of states has been the rule. In the crisis over

Chechnya, the United Nations and key governments treated the disproportionate Russian military action as an internal matter. Turkey and Burma, states with substantial numbers of internally displaced persons, have faced no challenge from the UN Security Council or agencies over their failure to accept either international scrutiny or assistance.

Such situations should no longer be ignored. It is time for the United Nations to develop procedures to deal more consistently and effectively with governments that obstruct urgently needed humanitarian assistance or shun UN representatives. The secretary-general and the heads of UN agencies should be prepared to intervene personally if necessary when states deliberately obstruct access or refuse it outright. Likewise, the secretary-general or the high commissioner for human rights should be prepared to step in when UN representatives or rapporteurs are denied entry to countries, as has frequently been the case for rapporteurs and in a few instances for the representative of the secretary-general on internally displaced persons.

The concept of sovereignty must include responsibility to one's citizens. In no case should states be allowed to use it as a screen behind which to hide mistreatment of their populations.

## Finally: Solutions

Can situations of mass internal displacement be resolved? If so, how? What are the solutions?

The starting point is recognition that providing humanitarian assistance alone cannot be expected to stabilize dangerous situations. Strictly palliative responses may simply help prolong a conflict, as in Sudan, where displacement remains unabated despite the fact that international humanitarian organizations and NGOs have operated relief programs for more than a decade.

When displacement is engendered by conflict, it is only through the restoration of peace accompanied by development programs that safe and viable returns or resettlement can be made possible. Moreover, to be effective, solutions for conflicts must promote respect for human rights and democratic participation and go hand in hand with programs to guarantee economic opportunity for the displaced and other affected populations.

## Return and Relocation

Serious problems can arise when internally displaced persons are compelled to return to unsafe areas or to areas where they do not wish to reside. Sudan once again offers an example: the government has forcibly moved the displaced from Khartoum to outlying areas where they are neither part of the urban community nor in their own natural setting. In Peru the government provides assistance only to those internally displaced persons who return to their original homes. In Sri Lanka, assistance has been used to induce returns, but to its credit the government has adopted guidelines against physical coercion. UN resolutions on the former Yugoslavia, Azerbaijan, and Georgia have stipulated a right of internally displaced persons and refugees to return in "safety and dignity." The Guiding Principles on Internal Displacement explicitly stipulate that returns should be voluntary and prohibit forcible returns to unsafe areas.

The provision of protection upon return also requires special attention. The return of the displaced to their home areas can be almost as difficult and fraught with danger as their initial displacement. They may find their homes, land, and personal property taken by others and no functioning judicial system to resolve disputes. Even when conflicts have subsided and peace agreements have been signed, there may be unsettled scores in villages and towns and a targeting of persons who return.

**Land mines kept displaced persons from returning to homes near Sarajevo long after fighting had stopped.**

Photograph by R. LeMoyne, Office of the UN High Commissioner for Refugees.

Consequently, in recent years humanitarian organizations, human rights field staff, NGOs, and peacekeeping forces have become directly involved in helping the displaced return. They have sought to foster reconciliation among different ethnic, religious, and racial communities and promote peaceful and equitable resolutions of land and property disputes. UNHCR has physically accompanied returnees home or arranged short trial visits to allow them to assess security for themselves. In Tajikistan the agency worked with local authorities to maximize physical security for returnees and has assisted returnees in reclaiming their homes. In Rwanda UN human rights field staff monitored conditions in areas of return and worked to ensure security.

Another serious problem returnees may face is land mines. In Mozambique these have killed more than 10,000 displaced persons over the course of the return and resettlement program. And tens of thousands more have been killed or maimed by land mines in Cambodia, the former Yugoslavia, Georgia, and Angola. Demining programs have been funded by the World Bank and others, and humanitarian and human rights agencies have sponsored awareness campaigns to alert returning populations to the danger of minefields. The Guiding Principles prohibit the deployment of land mines owing to the danger they pose to internally displaced and other civilians both during hostilities and after their conclusion.

### Linking Relief to Development

Another essential step in any program for solutions of internal displacement is the integration of relief with development. Traditionally, relief assistance was for the emergency stage; development assistance was timed to follow once the situation normalized. Increasingly, this traditional method has been found lacking. Displacement crises are often protracted. Return to normal cannot be expected simply because food and medical services are being supplied. Displaced populations need to maintain old skills and develop new ones if they are to become self-sustaining in their areas of displacement or upon return to their former homes.

Rather than a sequential continuum, what is needed is a parallelism in which the provision of emergency assistance and the planning of development programs take place simultaneously and in a mutually reinforcing manner. Under this concept, relief programs are designed to lay the foundation for development, and development-oriented programs are planned and initiated during the emergency phase. Tajikistan, where large parts of the rural and urban population remain dependent on relief supplies more than five years after its civil war ended, serves as a warning of what can happen if development programs are neglected or too long postponed.

In a community near Ayacucho, Peru, a local nongovernmental organization trains internally displaced youths in making traditional handicrafts, both as a means to involve them in constructive activities and to supplement their families' incomes.

Photograph by Hiram Ruiz, U.S. Committee for Refugees.

UNHCR's quick impact projects (QIPs), which aim to restore basic infrastructure and provide reintegration assistance for farming and small business enterprises for returning refugees and displaced persons, offer one solution. But to be sustainable, QIPs need to be linked with broader development initiatives and supported over a longer period of time. The UN Development Programme has earmarked $50 million for a rehabilitation fund for emergency situations. This should enable it to help uprooted populations in situations that do not meet traditional development criteria. Another promising initiative is the Framework for World Bank Involvement in Post Conflict Reconstruction, announced in May 1997, which names reintegration of displaced populations as one of the bank's new areas of activity.

But both the bank and other development institutions need strategies to guide their actions as they expand beyond traditional development activities. A major question they face is does the model established for Europe's post–World War II reconstruction have lessons to offer for rebuilding war-torn societies of the cold war and post–cold war eras? Or is another needed?

World Bank social scientist Steven Holtzman has contended that the strategy followed in reconstructing Europe's economies—repair of infrastructure and massive injection of investment capital—cannot be expected to work in the developing world. Conflicts in the 1980s and 1990s have been mainly internal. Some have gone on for decades and most have left in their wake severely fragmented societies and scars that may take generations to heal. There is often a widespread loss of skills among the displaced population, and for those whose only experience is working the land, the flight to urban centers makes the transition back to farming more difficult. Family units are sundered, gender roles altered, entire communities become marginalized, and trust in institutions is shattered. In short, internal conflicts break down the very underpinnings of society in countries that were poor in infrastructure and human capital to begin with.

**Internally displaced Azeri make stoves at an income-generating project sponsored by UNHCR at a displaced persons camp in Azerbaijan.**

Photograph by
R. Redmond,
Office of the UN High
Commissioner for
Refugees.

What can development agencies do to increase the capacity of communities to cope with displacement and enable displaced persons again to become self-supporting? The response varies at each stage.

*Conflict Prevention.* Breaking the cycle of conflict requires attention to its causes, particularly inequity in land holdings and competition for scarce resources. A World Bank paper identifies the following ways development investments can contribute to the prevention of conflict:

—through measures to reduce economic inequities and ensure reasonable equity in resource distribution within the society;

—through a participatory approach that engages and strengthens civil society;

—by promoting greater accountability and transparency on the part of governments in managing and distributing resources and providing legal and political frameworks for dispute resolution and conflict management; and

—through development programs designed to reduce violence and prevent displacement.[3]

*Development-Oriented Programs during Conflict.* The most important reason for development agencies to enter into conflict situations early is to initiate planning for a transition out of conflict. Transitions will be smoother if development agencies begin a partnership with relief agencies early in the crisis and get to understand the needs of displaced populations. Because the effects of conflict are rarely uniform throughout a country, QIPs

---

3. World Bank, "A Framework for World Bank Involvement in Post-Conflict Reconstruction," May 1997; and Steven Holtzman, "Conflict-Induced Displacement through a Development Lens," paper prepared for the Brookings Institution, May 1997.

and other development investments may be feasible in zones where active conflict is not occurring. The UN Development Fund for Women (UNIFEM) has found that training and income-earning activities can be successfully introduced in war-torn countries even though the requirements for traditional programs are not in place.

Other goals can be achieved as well. Programs that bolster the socioeconomic fabric of communities in conflict areas can reduce pressure on their members to flee, thereby preventing further displacement and easing the way to a stronger recovery. Experts from the UN Environmental Program (UNEP) could advise on the placement and design of displaced persons camps with a view to minimizing damage to the environment. Agronomists could work with relief agencies to minimize the impact of the distribution of food supplies so as to prevent the market for local agricultural production from collapsing. Most important is that relief and development investments focus on projects that will encourage the retention and development of skills so as to ease the burden on host communities and help prepare the displaced for return or resettlement.

*Postconflict Reconstruction.* When postconflict reconstruction fails, international donors are discouraged, confidence is undermined within the society, and the very professional and business people needed for reconstruction may leave. The providers of aid and those concerned with political negotiations need to coordinate closely to make certain that aid interventions support the negotiating process and do not inadvertently give advantage to one side or another. Aid programs also need to address the developmental problems that had beset the society before conflict broke out and may have contributed to its outbreak, particularly inequities in land distribution and weak infrastructure. Programs to demobilize, retrain, and reintegrate former combatants may be

**An internally displaced Bosnian Muslim woman works at carpet weaving at a UNHCR-sponsored women's center in Tuzla.**

Photograph by R. LeMoyne, Office of the UN High Commissioner for Refugees

necessary, along with removing land mines to allow access to transportation routes and the resumption of farming. Reconstruction efforts must also include programs to strengthen judicial systems, encourage pluralistic political frameworks, and safeguard human rights.

How to ensure funding for these programs? One solution would be to create an international trust fund in which donors could pool resources for the reintegration of displaced populations and the rebuilding of societies emerging from conflict.

Because women and their dependent children make up the bulk of internally displaced populations, and women are often left as the sole caretakers of their families, skills training and income-generating programs for them are essential. To be meaningful, these programs must go beyond teaching such traditional skills as sewing, embroidering, or making handicrafts. Women have shown themselves fully capable of working in nontraditional activities such as reforestation and other environmental and reconstruction projects. They should be included in large development projects undertaken in areas hosting refugee and displaced populations; and support services, in particular child care facilities, should be provided for them. The UNHCR has introduced gender clauses into quick-impact reintegration projects, stipulating that women receive equal pay with men and that up to 50 percent of the persons involved in the planning and implementation of the projects should be women. UNICEF, UNIFEM, and nongovernmental organizations likewise have sought to enlarge women's access to training and employment opportunities, but the scope of their programs is limited.

Cohen and Deng suggest that the World Bank target a share of its new $200 million microcredit program for internally displaced women who run small businesses. They call also for international efforts to revoke restrictions that exist in law in many countries on women's rights to own or inherit property and on their access to credit.

To sum up: by introducing development-oriented programs early in conflict situations, international development and financial institutions can help displaced populations make more manageable transitions out of conflict.

# Conclusion

In the aftermath of World War II the international community responded to the plight of masses in Europe who were forced to flee their countries and seek asylum in neighboring states. The measures taken led to legal and institutional arrangements for protection and assistance to refugees that remain a mainstay of the international humanitarian action system.

In the aftermath of the cold war the world faces a crisis of internal displacement that is no less acute and pressing than the refugee crisis. The international community can no more afford to ignore today's masses in flight than it could those of yesterday. The numbers are greater. In human rights and humanitarian terms their situation may be even more critical. The victims are trapped inside state borders under conditions of internal conflict, communal violence, and terrible violations of human rights. And the crises engendered frequently spill across borders and can spread violence and instability over entire regions.

Readers who wish to learn more about this important subject should consult Roberta Cohen and Francis Deng's landmark study, *Masses in Flight*, and its companion volume, *The Forsaken*

*People*. Years in preparation and with information and observations from many experts and nongovernmental organizations, the books offer an in-depth look at the issues raised by today's global crises of internal displacement. Each of these issues is complex, and none has simple, easy solutions. They require engagement at all levels—local, national, regional, and international. And they can succeed only through strong leadership by the United Nations and regional organizations.

The crises of displacement since the end of the cold war differs from that of the post–World War II years in fundmental ways. Today displacement, both internal and external, is almost exclusively the product of civil wars or domestic disturbances. Unlike wars among nations, civil wars, particularly when they involve competing ethnic, linguistic, or religious communities, do not come to neat, easily defined conclusions. Often they recur, and they can drag out for decades. They leave deep cleavages that cannot be healed simply by providing emergency relief and then development assistance. These efforts must be integrated, and there must also be mechanisms for prevention, protection, reintegration, and political conciliation. And along the way there arise troubling issues of state sovereignty.

Essentially, much of the difficulty the international community has encountered in meeting the challenges of the post–cold war era stem from its having to do so with a humanitarian response system shaped both in its institutions and its methods by the experience and the needs of an earlier time. That system, which operated with reasonable effectiveness in Europe after World War II and during the cold war years, has shown itself to be poorly adapted for dealing with the very different worldwide crisis of internal displacement of the 1990s. In consequence, both within the United Nations and outside it planners have begun to rethink the system's legal, institutional, and operational norms.

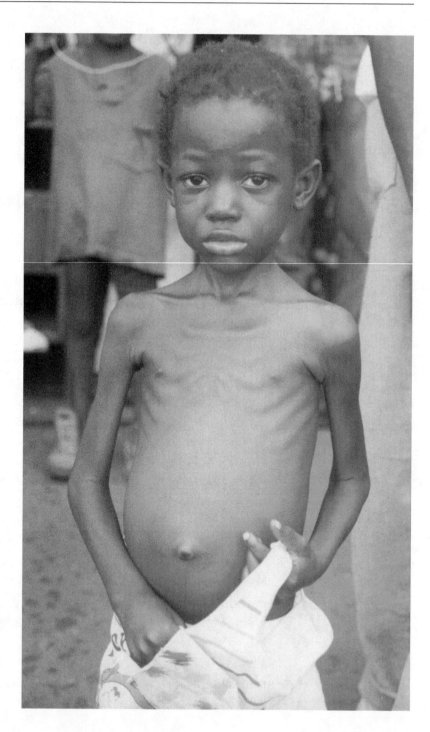

**Child displaced by
the outbreak of civil
war in Liberia;
Monrovia, 1990.**

Photograph by Hiram Ruiz,
U.S. Committee for
Refugees.

*Masses in Flight* is part of that process. On the legal side it offers principles to guide the action both of governments and of international humanitarian and development agencies in dealing with crises of internal displacement. It advocates the proposition—essential if there is ever to be a just and stable international order—that a state that fails to live up to the responsibilities of sovereignty in its dealings with its citizens forfeits its prerogatives and legitimizes international action to assist and protect the people. Operationally, it makes a range of suggestions, stressing in particular the urgent need to improve protection for the internally displaced and bring international human rights agencies into an operational mode.

On the matter of institutional reform no radical new solution is in prospect. The creation of a new agency to deal with internal displacement, while attractive in theory, in reality would face both practical and political obstacles that would be difficult to overcome. Assigning responsibility to a single existing agency seems equally unlikely. Accordingly, the international community has little current choice but to settle for incremental efforts to promote a more effective collaborative approach among the existing humanitarian and development agencies that deal with internal displacement.

The challenge is to find ways to overcome the notorious problems of coordination, bureaucratic torpor, tendency toward turf protection, and agency rivalries that together with the chronic shortage of funding have so far obstructed the collaborative system's performance. A mere reshuffling of institutional responsibility within the United Nations is not in itself a panacea. To be effective, it must be accompanied by the adoption of comprehensive strategies that in addition to humanitarian relief encompass prevention of displacement, protection of internally displaced persons, political initiatives to resolve conflicts, and measures for reintegration and development of the displaced. And by a dedication to making the strategies work.

There is reason for optimism. UN Secretary-General Kofi Annan has given formal recognition to internal displacement as one of the gaps in the international humanitarian response system. UN Emergency Relief Coordinator Sergio Vieira de Mello has committed himself to strengthening the UN's response to crises of internal displacement by promoting better coordination, a clearer division of responsibilities, and support for the Guiding Principles on Internal Displacement. Setting aside early hesitations, UN and other international humanitarian and human rights agency heads and staff have come to accord high priority to crises of internal displacement both in planning and in operations.

They merit the unreserved support, both political and, where necessary, military, of donor governments and regional bodies, for much hangs on their collective success. As the authors of *Masses in Flight* write in the closing lines of their study:

A world in which the privileged among nations ignore the plight of the unfortunate can be neither prosperous nor safe for anyone.

# Guiding Principles on Internal Displacement

## Introduction: Scope and Purpose

1. These Guiding Principles address the specific needs of internally displaced persons worldwide. They identify rights and guarantees relevant to the protection of persons from forced displacement and to their protection and assistance during displacement as well as during return or resettlement and reintegration.

2. For the purposes of these Principles, internally displaced persons are persons or groups of persons who have been forced or obliged to flee or to leave their homes or places of habitual residence, in particular as a result of or in order to avoid the effects of armed conflict, situations of generalized violence, violations of human rights or natural or human-made disasters, and who have not crossed an internationally recognized state border.

3. These Principles reflect and are consistent with international human rights law and international humanitarian law. They provide guidance to:

    (a)  The Representative of the Secretary-General on internally displaced persons in carrying out his mandate;

    (b)  States when faced with the phenomenon of internal displacement;

(c)   All other authorities, groups and persons in their relations with internally displaced persons; and

(d) Intergovernmental and non-governmental organizations when addressing internal displacement.

4. These Guiding Principles should be disseminated and applied as widely as possible.

## Section I: General Principles

### Principle 1

1. Internally displaced persons shall enjoy, in full equality, the same rights and freedoms under international and domestic law as do other persons in their country. They shall not be discriminated against in the enjoyment of any rights and freedoms on the ground that they are internally displaced.

2. These Principles are without prejudice to individual criminal responsibility under international law, in particular relating to genocide, crimes against humanity and war crimes.

### Principle 2

1: These Principles shall be observed by all authorities, groups and persons irrespective of their legal status and applied without any adverse distinction. The observance of these Principles shall not affect the legal status of any authorities, groups or persons involved.

2. These Principles shall not be interpreted as restricting, modifying or impairing the provisions of any international human rights or international humanitarian law instrument or rights granted to persons under domestic law. In particular, these Principles are without prejudice to the right to seek and enjoy asylum in other countries.

### Principle 3

1. National authorities have the primary duty and responsibility to provide protection and humanitarian assistance to internally displaced persons within their jurisdiction.

2. Internally displaced persons have the right to request and to receive protection and humanitarian assistance from these authorities. They shall not be persecuted or punished for making such a request.

### Principle 4

1. These Principles shall be applied without discrimination of any kind, such as race, color, sex, language, religion or belief, political or other opinion, national, ethnic or social origin, legal or social status, age, disability, property, birth, or on any other similar criteria.

2. Certain internally displaced persons, such as children, especially unaccompanied minors, expectant mothers, mothers with young children, female heads of household, persons with disabilities and elderly persons, shall be entitled to protection and assistance required by their condition and to treatment which takes into account their special needs.

## Section II: Principles Relating to Protection from Displacement

### Principle 5

All authorities and international actors shall respect and ensure respect for their obligations under international law, including human rights and humanitarian law, in all circumstances, so as to prevent and avoid conditions that might lead to displacement of persons.

### Principle 6

1. Every human being shall have the right to be protected against being arbitrarily displaced from his or her home or place of habitual residence.

2. The prohibition of arbitrary displacement includes displacement:

   (a) When it is based on policies of apartheid, "ethnic cleansing" or similar practices aimed at/or resulting in altering the ethnic, religious or racial composition of the affected population;

   (b) In situations of armed conflict, unless the security of the civilians involved or imperative military reasons so demand;

   (c) In cases of large-scale development projects, which are not justified by compelling and overriding public interests;

   (d) In cases of disasters, unless the safety and health of those affected requires their evacuation; and

   (e) When it is used as a collective punishment.

3. Displacement shall last no longer than required by the circumstances.

### Principle 7

1. Prior to any decision requiring the displacement of persons, the authorities concerned shall ensure that all feasible alternatives are explored in order to avoid displacement altogether. Where no alternatives exist, all measures shall be taken to minimise displacement and its adverse effects.

2. The authorities undertaking such displacement shall ensure, to the greatest practicable extent, that proper accommodation is provided to the displaced persons, that such displacements are effected in satisfactory conditions of safety, nutrition,

health and hygiene, and that members of the same family are not separated.

3. If displacement occurs in situations other than during the emergency stages of armed conflicts and disasters, the following guarantees shall be complied with:

(a) A specific decision shall be taken by a State authority empowered by law to order such measures;

(b) Adequate measures shall be taken to guarantee to those to be displaced full information on the reasons and procedures for their displacement and, where applicable, on compensation and relocation;

(c) The free and informed consent of those to be displaced shall be sought;

(d) The authorities concerned shall endeavor to involve those affected, particularly women, in the planning and management of their relocation;

(e) Law enforcement measures, where required, shall be carried out by competent legal authorities; and

(f) The right to an effective remedy, including the review of such decisions by appropriate judicial authorities, shall be respected.

## Principle 8

Displacement shall not be carried out in a manner that violates the rights to life, dignity, liberty and security of those affected.

## Principle 9

States are under a particular obligation to protect against the displacement of indigenous peoples, minorities, peasants, pastoralists and other groups with a special dependency on and attachment to their lands.

## Section III: Principles Relating to Protection During Displacement

### Principle 10

1. Every human being has the inherent right to life which shall be protected by law. No one shall be arbitrarily deprived of his or her life. Internally displaced persons shall be protected in particular against:

    (a) Genocide;

    (b) Murder;

    (c) Summary or arbitrary executions; and

    (d) Enforced disappearances, including abduction or unacknowledged detention, threatening or resulting in death.

Threats and incitement to commit any of the foregoing acts shall be prohibited.

2. Attacks or other acts of violence against internally displaced persons who do not or no longer participate in hostilities are prohibited in all circumstances. Internally displaced persons shall be protected, in particular, against:

    (a) Direct or indiscriminate attacks or other acts of violence, including the creation of areas wherein attacks on civilians are permitted;

    (b) Starvation as a method of combat;

    (c) Their use to shield military objectives from attack or to shield, favor or impede military operations;

    (d) Attacks against their camps or settlements; and

    (e) The use of anti-personnel landmines.

### Principle 11

1. Every human being has the right to dignity and physical, mental and moral integrity.

2. Internally displaced persons, whether or not their liberty has been restricted, shall be protected in particular against:

(a) Rape, mutilation, torture, cruel, inhuman or degrading treatment or punishment, and other outrages upon personal dignity, such as acts of gender-specific violence, forced prostitution and any form of indecent assault;

(b) Slavery or any contemporary form of slavery, such as sale into marriage, sexual exploitation, or forced labor of children; and

(c) Acts of violence intended to spread terror among internally displaced persons.

Threats and incitement to commit any of the foregoing acts shall be prohibited.

### Principle 12

1. Every human being has the right to liberty and security of person. No one shall be subjected to arbitrary arrest or detention.

2. To give effect to this right for internally displaced persons, they shall not be interned in or confined to a camp. If in exceptional circumstances such internment or confinement is absolutely necessary, it shall not last longer than required by the circumstances.

3. Internally displaced persons shall be protected from discriminatory arrest and detention as a result of their displacement.

4. In no case shall internally displaced persons be taken hostage.

### Principle 13

1. In no circumstances shall displaced children be recruited nor be required or permitted to take part in hostilities.

2. Internally displaced persons shall be protected against discriminatory practices of recruitment into any armed forces or

groups as a result of their displacement. In particular any cruel, inhuman or degrading practices that compel compliance or punish non-compliance with recruitment are prohibited in all circumstances.

### Principle 14

1. Every internally displaced person has the right to liberty of movement and freedom to choose his or her residence.

2. In particular, internally displaced persons have the right to move freely in and out of camps or other settlements.

### Principle 15

Internally displaced persons have:

(a) The right to seek safety in another part of the country;

(b) The right to leave their country;

(c) The right to seek asylum in another country; and

(d) The right to be protected against forcible return to or resettlement in any place where their life, safety, liberty and/or health would be at risk.

### Principle 16

1. All internally displaced persons have the right to know the fate and whereabouts of missing relatives.

2. The authorities concerned shall endeavor to establish the fate and whereabouts of internally displaced persons reported missing, and cooperate with relevant international organizations engaged in this task. They shall inform the next of kin on the progress of the investigation and notify them of any result.

3. The authorities concerned shall endeavor to collect and identify the mortal remains of those deceased, prevent their despoliation or mutilation, and facilitate the return of those remains to the next of kin or dispose of them respectfully.

4. Grave sites of internally displaced persons should be protected and respected in all circumstances. Internally displaced persons should have the right of access to the grave sites of their deceased relatives.

**Principle 17**

1. Every human being has the right to respect of his or her family life.

2. To give effect to this right for internally displaced persons, family members who wish to remain together shall be allowed to do so.

3. Families which are separated by displacement should be reunited as quickly as possible. All appropriate steps shall be taken to expedite the reunion of such families, particularly when children are involved. The responsible authorities shall facilitate inquiries made by family members and encourage and cooperate with the work of humanitarian organizations engaged in the task of family reunification.

4. Members of internally displaced families whose personal liberty has been restricted by internment or confinement in camps shall have the right to remain together.

**Principle 18**

1. All internally displaced persons have the right to an adequate standard of living.

2. At the minimum, regardless of the circumstances, and without discrimination, competent authorities shall provide internally displaced persons with and ensure safe access to:

  (a) Essential food and potable water;
  (b) Basic shelter and housing;
  (c) Appropriate clothing; and
  (d) Essential medical services and sanitation.

3. Special efforts should be made to ensure the full participation of women in the planning and distribution of these basic supplies.

### Principle 19

1. All wounded and sick internally displaced persons as well as those with disabilities shall receive to the fullest extent practicable and with the least possible delay, the medical care and attention they require, without distinction on any grounds other than medical ones. When necessary, internally displaced persons shall have access to psychological and social services.

2. Special attention should be paid to the health needs of women, including access to female health care providers and services, such as reproductive health care, as well as appropriate counseling for victims of sexual and other abuses.

3. Special attention should also be given to the prevention of contagious and infectious diseases, including AIDS, among internally displaced persons.

### Principle 20

1. Every human being has the right to recognition everywhere as a person before the law.

2. To give effect to this right for internally displaced persons, the authorities concerned shall issue to them all documents necessary for the enjoyment and exercise of their legal rights, such as passports, personal identification documents, birth certificates and marriage certificates. In particular, the authorities shall facilitate the issuance of new documents or the replacement of documents lost in the course of displacement, without imposing unreasonable conditions, such as requiring the return to one's area of habitual residence in order to obtain these or other required documents.

3. Women and men shall have equal rights to obtain such necessary documents and shall have the right to have such documentation issued in their own names.

**Principle 21**

1. No one shall be arbitrarily deprived of property and possessions.

2. The property and possessions of internally displaced persons shall in all circumstances be protected, in particular, against the following acts:

    (a) Pillage;

    (b) Direct or indiscriminate attacks or other acts of violence;

    (c) Being used to shield military operations or objectives;

    (d) Being made the object of reprisal; and

    (e) Being destroyed or appropriated as a form of collective punishment.

3. Property and possessions left behind by internally displaced persons should be protected against destruction and arbitrary and illegal appropriation, occupation or use.

**Principle 22**

1. Internally displaced persons, whether or not they are living in camps, shall not be discriminated against as a result of their displacement in the enjoyment of the following rights:

    (a) The rights to freedom of thought, conscience, religion or belief, opinion and expression;

    (b) The right to seek freely opportunities for employment and to participate in economic activities;

    (c) The right to associate freely and participate equally in community affairs;

    (d) The right to vote and to participate in governmental and public affairs, including the right to have access to the means necessary to exercise this right; and

    (e) The right to communicate in a language they understand.

**Principle 23**

1. Every human being has the right to education.

2. To give effect to this right for internally displaced persons, the authorities concerned shall ensure that such persons, in particular displaced children, receive education which shall be free and compulsory at the primary level. Education should respect their cultural identity, language and religion.

3. Special efforts should be made to ensure the full and equal participation of women and girls in educational programmes.

4. Education and training facilities shall be made available to internally displaced persons, in particular adolescents and women, whether or not living in camps, as soon as conditions permit.

## Section IV: Principles Relating to Humanitarian Assistance

### Principle 24

1. All humanitarian assistance shall be carried out in accordance with the principles of humanity and impartiality and without discrimination.

2. Humanitarian assistance to internally displaced persons shall not be diverted, in particular for political or military reasons.

### Principle 25

1. The primary duty and responsibility for providing humanitarian assistance to internally displaced persons lies with national authorities.

2. International humanitarian organizations and other appropriate actors have the right to offer their services in support of the internally displaced. Such an offer shall not be regarded as an unfriendly act or an interference in a State's internal affairs and shall be considered in good faith. Consent thereto shall not be arbitrarily withheld, particularly when authorities concerned are unable or unwilling to provide the required humanitarian assistance.

3. All authorities concerned shall grant and facilitate the free passage of humanitarian assistance and grant persons engaged in the provision of such assistance rapid and unimpeded access to the internally displaced.

## Principle 26

Persons engaged in humanitarian assistance, their transports and supplies shall be respected and protected. They shall not be the object of attack or other acts of violence.

## Principle 27

1. International humanitarian organizations and other appropriate actors when providing assistance should give due regard to the protection needs and human rights of internally displaced persons and take appropriate measures in this regard. In so doing, these organizations and actors should respect relevant international standards and codes of conduct.

2. The preceding paragraph is without prejudice to the protection responsibilities of international organizations mandated for this purpose, whose services may be offered or requested by States.

## Section V: Principles Relating to Return, Resettlement and Reintegration

## Principle 28

1. Competent authorities have the primary duty and responsibility to establish conditions, as well as provide the means, which allow internally displaced persons to return voluntarily, in safety and with dignity, to their homes or places of habitual residence, or to resettle voluntarily in another part of the country. Such author-

ities shall endeavor to facilitate the reintegration of returned or resettled internally displaced persons.

2. Special efforts should be made to ensure the full participation of internally displaced persons in the planning and management of their return or resettlement and reintegration.

## Principle 29

1. Internally displaced persons who have returned to their homes or places of habitual residence or who have resettled in another part of the country shall not be discriminated against as a result of their having been displaced. They shall have the right to participate fully and equally in public affairs at all levels and have equal access to public services.

2. Competent authorities have the duty and responsibility to assist returned and/or resettled internally displaced persons to recover, to the extent possible, their property and possessions which they left behind or were dispossessed of upon their displacement. When recovery of such property and possessions is not possible, competent authorities shall provide or assist these persons in obtaining appropriate compensation or another form of just reparation.

## Principle 30

All authorities concerned shall grant and facilitate for international humanitarian organizations and other appropriate actors, in the exercise of their respective mandates, rapid and unimpeded access to internally displaced persons to assist in their return or resettlement and reintegration.

# Index